D0000143

Blessings
for
Sacred
Moments

Simple Blessings *for* Sacred Moments

A COLLECTION BY
ISABEL ANDERS

LIGUORI/TRIUMPH
LIGUORI, MISSOURI

Published by Liguori/Triumph
An Imprint of Liguori Publications
Liguori, Missouri

Library of Congress Cataloging-in-Publication Data

Anders, Isabel, 1946–

    Simple blessings for sacred moments / a collection by
Isabel Anders. — 1st ed.
      p. cm.
    ISBN 0-7648-0221-6
    1. Benedictionals. I. Title
BV199.B4A53   1998
242'.8—dc21   98–17287

Printed in the United States of America
02 01 00 99 98 5 4 3 2 1
First Edition

TO SARAH ALISON

ACKNOWLEDGMENTS

I want to acknowledge the invaluable help and support of my editor, Judy Bauer, who conceived this concept, guided its direction, and aided all phases of the project with clarity, intelligence, and a wonderful spirit.

And a special thanks to KiKi Crombie, for her significant contribution to this work: her encouragement, her ideas, her understanding—and most of all, her friendship.

I also want to thank Paula Franck, Coordinator of the Congregational Resource Center, Christian Theological Seminary, Indianapolis, Indiana, for her fine research and contributions to this book.

CONTENTS

Contents

Contents

PREFACE

Collecting, compiling, adapting, writing portions of a book of blessings to share with a wider community has been for me a rich and enlarging experience. It is like finding oneself in a garden of language, all directed toward the building up, enlightening, and blessing of each other's daily lives and spirits.

First of all, to all those other minds and hearts who have made this book possible, I extend a spirit of blessing across time and distance. I am humbly honored at the opportunity that has been afforded me to compile *Simple Blessings for Sacred Moments*.

As a Christian, my criterion for choosing and including blessings has been: *Can this be presented and prayed to my Lord and on behalf of others?* To me, the spirit of Christ shines through the truths on these pages, sometimes in explicit and often in more veiled expressions of the source of Truth—which for me is God in Christ.

No book of this sort can ever be "complete"; but we have striven to include topics intended to be used to bless times and seasons, milestones and everyday life—many of which can be applied to quite variant situations. Effort has been made to give credit and recognition wherever possible.

When Jesus said to "Bless those who curse you" (Luke 6:28) (compare Matthew 5:44: "Pray for those who persecute you"; and "Bless and do not curse them," Romans 12:14)—he did not mean simply to find a suitable chain of positive words and pronounce them over such a person. Rather, blessing one another—honoring all creatures—in the spirit of Christ, is a way of life. The words (whether spontaneous or written, simple or intellectually complex) are merely the plant rising above the surface to flower. The blessing of others—and of oneself—always begins in the heart.

Yet words have power. The prayers and consecrations and blessings that we share in a community of believers set in motion real events, and alter attitudes, when hearts are open to God's real presence among us. In blessing others, we also bless ourselves, unite ourselves to these others, and find unity in one Lord, one faith.

I believe that positive, encouraging, truthful, words spoken in any context can produce real fruit in others' lives—especially when they are truly a gift to another and not (even subconsciously) a desire to flatter or manipulate. The effect of a sincere blessing on a sick person, or of a child on her birthday, or of a person beginning new work—or a request for God to dwell in a new home with its occupants—can be profound. It is like the stone thrown into the pool of water that rings out its effects immeasurably. So, bless often, appropriately, thoughtfully, and with as much faith as you yourself can bring to the situation. *Make blessing others your way of life.* Thus you become and remain part of the circle of love, of which God is always the center.

What about blessings that don't mention God? For the Christian there can be a sense of prayer in actions and words and thoughts without specifically religious language. Sometimes such God-words are timely, and at other times we simply radiate God by being there at all, by blessing from our own hearts, which belong to God in the first place.

And so I present these prayers, blessings, and insights on the process of blessing others—for use by individuals and groups, in silence and in joyful celebrations...for use throughout the year and years.

When in doubt, bless!

ISABEL ANDERS

Simple
Blessings
for
Sacred
Moments

Part I

—

Daily
Blessings

Morning Blessings

Lord, catch us off guard today. Surprise us with some moment of beauty or pain so that for at least a moment we may be startled into seeing that you are with us here in all your splendor, always and everywhere, barely hidden, beneath, beyond, within this life we breathe.

FREDERICK BUECHNER

Blessed art You, who removes sleep from mine eyes,
yea, and slumber from mine eyelids.
Blessed art You, who restores life to mortal creatures.

JEWISH MORNING PRAYER

Living Lord, you have watched over me, and put your hand on my head, during the long, dark hours of night. Your holy angels have protected me from all harm and pain. To you, Lord, I owe life itself. Continue to watch over me and bless me during the hours of day.

JACOB BOEHME (1575–1624)

Dear God,
As we rise up this morning, open your doors
    of mercy,
Hear our prayer and have mercy upon
    our souls.
Lord of the morning and ruler of the seasons:
Hear our prayer and have mercy
    upon our souls.
Shine on us, Lord, and make us light
    like the day.
Let your light shine in our minds and
        drive away
    the shadows of error and night.
The creation is full of light,
    give your light also to our hearts
    that we may praise you all the long day.
The morning and the evening praise
    you, Lord.
They bring you the praise of your people.
O Light who gives light to all creatures;
Give light to our minds that we may
    thank you.
Amen.

SYRIAN ORTHODOX LITURGY

Thanks to You, O God, that I have
    risen today.
To the rising of this life itself;
May it be to Your own glory,
O God of every gift,
And to the glory of my soul likewise.
O great God, and you my soul
with the aiding of Your own mercy;
Even as I clothe my body with wool,
Cover my soul with the shadow of Your wing.
Help me to avoid every sin,
and the source of every sin to forsake;
And as the mist scatters on the crest
    of the hills,
may each ill haze clear from my soul, O God.

GAELIC GRACE (19TH CENTURY)

Grant us, Lord, to pass this day in gladness
    and in peace
without stumbling and without stain;
That, reaching the eventide
    victorious over all temptation,
We may praise you, the eternal God,
Who is blessed, and who governs all things,
World without end.

MOZARABIC LITURGY

O God, our Creator and our Father, who has given unto us the gift of life, bless us this day as we go to the work which has been given unto us to do.

Help us today to be cheerful, that it may make others happier to meet us. Help us to be so true to You, that we may be a strength to others who are tempted.

O Lord Jesus, we have begun the day with You; grant that Your reflection may be upon us throughout all its hours. Amen.

WILLIAM BARCLAY

Blessing on Making the Bed

This bed I make
In the name of the Father, and of the Son, and of the Holy Spirit;
In the name of the night we were conceived;
In the name of the day we were baptized;
In the name of every night, every day,
   every season,
And of every angel that is in Heaven.

GAELIC BLESSING

Blessing on
Getting Dressed

Merciful God, you clothed your Word with the pure and perfect body of our Lord Jesus. Clothe my soul with that same purity, that I may share his perfection. Yet at his passion our Lord Jesus was stripped, and on the cross his earthly body killed. Thus my own body can only be clothed in purity if my sins are stripped and laid bare, and then nailed to the cross. Dear God, destroy my sins, and so make me ready to put on the cloak of eternal life.

JACOB BOEHME (1575–1624)

Noon Blessings

May the blessing of light be on you, light without and light within. May the blessed sunshine shine on you and warm your heart till it glows like a great peat fire, so that the stranger may come and warm himself at it, and also a friend.

And may the light shine out of the two eyes of you, like a candle set in the two windows of a house, bidding the wanderer come in out of the storm. And may the blessings of the rain be on you—the soft, sweet rain. May it fall upon your spirit so that all the little flowers may spring up and shed their sweetness on the air....

And may the blessing of the Earth be on you—the great round earth; may you ever have a kindly greeting for those you pass as you're going along the roads.

IRISH BLESSING

In the name of Jesus Christ, who was never in a hurry, we pray, O God, that You will slow us down, for we know that we live too fast. With all of eternity before us, make us take time to live—time to get acquainted with You, time to enjoy Your blessings, and time to know each other.

PETER MARSHALL (1902–1949)

O God, creation's secret force,
Thyself unmoved, all motion's source;
Who, from the morn till evening's ray,
Through all its changes guid'st the day.

Come, Holy Ghost, with God the Son,
And God the Father ever one;
Shed forth thy grace within our breast,
And dwell with us a ready guest.

By every power, by heart and tongue,
By act and deed thy praise be sung;
Inflame with perfect love each sense
That others' souls may kindle thence.

A NEW ZEALAND PRAYER BOOK
"A HYMN FOR MIDDAY"

Evening Blessings

Watch out for evening temptations. Do not think you are secure....We need a watchman at night as well as a guardian during the day. *O blessed Spirit, keep us from evil tonight. Amen.*

CHARLES SPURGEON (1834–1892)

Do not look forward to what may happen tomorrow; the same everlasting Father who cares for you today will take care of you tomorrow and every day. Either He will shield you from suffering, or He will give you unfailing strength to bear it.

Be at peace, then, put aside all anxious thoughts and imaginations, and say continually: "The Lord is my strength and my shield; my heart has trusted in Him and I am helped. He is not only with me but in me and I in Him."

SAINT FRANCIS DE SALES (1567–1622)

Lord, it is night.
The night is for stillness.
 Let us be still in the presence of God.
It is night after a long day.
 What has been done has been done;
 what has not been done has not been done;
 let it be.

The night is dark.
 Let our fears of the darkness of the world
 and of our own lives
 rest in you.

The night is quiet.
 Let the quietness of your peace enfold us,
 all dear to us,
 and all who have no peace.

The night heralds the dawn.
 Let us look expectantly to a new day,
 new joys, new possibilities.

In your name we pray. Amen.
 A NEW ZEALAND PRAYER BOOK

O God, Light of lights,
Keep us from inward darkness.
Grant us so to sleep in peace,
that we may arise to work according
to Your Will.

LANCELOT ANDREWES (1555–1626)

To the God of life, the God of peace and the
God of grace, we pray:

> Save us
> Shield us
> Surround this hearth
> This house
> This household on this eve
> This night...
> And on every night
> Each single night.
> Amen.

RUNE OF THE PEAT FIRE,
TRADITIONAL IRISH PRAYER

The sun has disappeared,
I have switched off the light,
and my wife and children are asleep.
The animals in the forest are full of fear,
and so are the people on their mats.
They prefer the day with your sun
   to the night.
But I still know that your moon is there,
and your eyes and also your hands.
Thus I am not afraid.

This day again
you led us wonderfully.
Everybody went to his mat
satisfied and full.
Renew us during our sleep,
that in the morning
we may come afresh to our daily jobs.

PRAYER FROM GHANA

May the Earth be soft under you when you rest upon it, tired at the end of a day, and may it rest easy over you when at the last you lay out under it; may it rest so lightly over you that your soul may be off from under it quickly and up and off, and on its way to God. And now may the Lord bless you all and bless you kindly.

TRADITIONAL IRISH BLESSING

———

I reverently speak in the presence
    of the Great Parent God.
I give You grateful thanks
that You have enabled me to live this day,
    the whole day,
in obedience to the excellent spirit
    of Your ways.

SHINTO EVENING PRAYER

———

Save us, Lord, while waking, and guard us while sleeping, that when we wake, we may watch with Christ, and when we sleep we may rest in peace.

ROMAN BREVIARY

The day that has passed has been full of temptations. I have yielded to numerous distractions, and forgotten Your law. I have fallen into the petty thralldom of little sins, evasions and indulgences. Deliver me, O Lord: Let the night's rest restore me. Into Your hand I commit my spirit, and in You I put my trust. You will redeem me, O God of Truth. Amen.

TRADITIONAL PRAYER

Father in Heaven! Our thought is turned toward You; again it seeks You at this hour, not with the unsteady step of a lost traveler but with the sure flight of a bird homeward bound. Grant that our aspirations toward Your Kingdom, our hopes for Your glory, be not unproductive birth pangs or waterless clouds, but that from the fullness of our heart they will rise toward You, and that being heard they will quench our thirst like the refreshing dew and satisfy us forever like Your heavenly manna.

SØREN KIERKEGAARD (1813–1855)

O Lord our God, what sins I have this day committed in word, deed, or thought, forgive me, for You are most gracious, and love all people. Grant me peaceful and undisturbed sleep, send me Your guardian angel to protect and guard me from every evil, for You are the guardian of our souls and bodies, and to You we ascribe glory, to the Father and the Son and the Holy Ghost, now and for ever and unto the ages of ages.

RUSSIAN ORTHODOX PRAYER

The angels of God guard us through
    the night,
and quiet the powers of darkness.
The Spirit of God be our guide
to lead us to peace and to glory.
It is but lost labor that we haste
    to rise up early,
and so late take rest, and eat the bread
    of anxiety.
For those beloved of God are given gifts
    even while they sleep.

A NEW ZEALAND PRAYER BOOK

Throughout all generations we will render
    thanks unto You, O God,
And declare Your praise,
Evening, morning, and noon,
For our lives which are in Your care,
For our souls which are in Your keeping,
For Your miracles which we witness daily,
And for Your wondrous deeds
    and blessings toward us
    at all times.

JEWISH SABBATH EVENING PRAYER

O Lord God, who has given us the night for rest, I pray that in my sleep my soul may remain awake to you, steadfastly adhering to your love. As I lay aside my cares to relax and relieve my mind, may I not forget your infinite and unresting care for me. And in this way, let my conscience be at peace, so that when I rise tomorrow, I am refreshed in body, mind and soul.

JOHN CALVIN (1509–1564)

Blessings on Meal Preparation

Lord of the pots and pipkins, since I have no time to be a saint by doing lovely things and vigiling with Thee, by watching in the twilight dawn, and storming Heaven's gates, make me a saint by getting meals, and washing up the plates!

Warm all the kitchen with Thy love, and light it with Thy peace;

Forgive me all my worrying, and make all grumbling cease. Thou who did so love to give men food, in room or by the sea, accept this service that I do—I do it unto thee.

CECILY HALLACK

I possess God as tranquilly in the bustle of my kitchen...as if I were on my knees before the Blessed Sacrament.... It is not necessary to have great things to do. I turn my little omelet in the pan for the love of God....When I cannot do anything else, it is enough for me to have lifted a straw from the earth for the love of God.

BROTHER LAWRENCE (1611–1691)

Cooking for the love of God, the cook realizes the importance of his work for others. When others eat what you have cooked, biological, psychological, social, and spiritual needs may be met. People can become both physically and psychologically hungry. Sometimes it is good to question or ask which. Perhaps a meal made from your listening ears is needed. When cooking with awareness of those who will eat, and in the context of "preparing spirit," the actions of the cook become love. Again, this love is always a prayer, one that can unceasingly flow from the kitchen.

PHILIP MAGALETTA

———

Each thought, each action in the sunlight of awareness becomes sacred. I must confess it takes me a bit longer to do the dishes, but I live fully in every moment, and I am happy.

T. H. HANH

Blessings at Table

When we share some bread and some wine together, we do this not as people who have arrived, but as men and women who can support each other in patient expectation until we see Jesus again. And then our hearts will be full of joy, a joy that no one can take away from us.

HENRI J. M. NOUWEN (1932–1996)

———

Lord, may our fellowship be the revelation of your presence and turn our daily bread into bread of life.

ALTERNATIVE SERVICE BOOK, ANGLICAN CHURCH OF CANADA

———

Come, Lord Jesus, be our guest,
And may our meal by thee be blest.

ATTRIBUTED TO MARTIN LUTHER (1483–1546)

Bless, O Lord, this food for our use,
and our lives to your loving service.
Give us grateful hearts, and keep us
ever mindful of the needs
and feelings of others. Amen.

———

Our heavenly Father, You have provided us
with all good things, so fill our hearts with Your
love and grace that we may use every gift to Your
greater glory. Amen.

TRADITIONAL TABLE BLESSING

———

O Lord, in a world where many are lonely: we
thank you for our friendships. In a world where
many are captive, we thank you for our freedom. In a world where many are hungry, we
thank you for our provisions. We pray that you
will enlarge our sympathy, deepen our compassion, and give us grateful hearts. In Christ's
name. Amen.

TERRY WAITE

Lord of the Meal,
  we come to this prayer called grace
  asking that You help us eat this food
  gracefully
  and with gratitude;
  that we, with grace and care,
  share our lives by word and laughter,
May Your grace, Your life
  touch us and our food.

We lift up this bread *(lift up bread),*
  symbol of life and of Your Son;
  may it and He nourish us this day.
  Amen.
  EDWARD HAYS

———

Blessed be God, who in his mercy nourishes us from his bounteous gifts by his grace and compassion. O Christ, our God, bless the meat and drink of which we are about to partake, for you are holy forever. Amen.
  EASTERN ORTHODOX BLESSING

Bless me, O Lord, and let my food strengthen me to serve You, for Jesus Christ's sake. Amen.

ISAAC WATTS (1674–1748)

———

Be present at our table, Lord;
Be here and everywhere adored.
Bless your creatures, and grant that we
May feast in paradise with thee.

JOHN WESLEY (1703–1791)

———

We cannot love God unless we love each other, and to love each other we must know each other in the breaking of bread...and then we are not alone anymore. Heaven is a banquet—and life is a banquet, too, even with a crust, where there is companionship. Love comes with community. Grant us, O Lord, the love that comes with the breaking of bread.

DOROTHY DAY (1897–1980)

Reveal Your presence now, O Lord,
As in the upper room of old;
    Break You our bread,
    Grace You our board,
And keep our hearts from growing cold.
ANCIENT PRAYER

May the Three-in-One bless those things
which we are about to eat.
INSCRIBED IN LATIN ON A
16TH-CENTURY KNIFE AT THE LOUVRE

O God, bless this food we are about to receive.
Give bread to those who hunger; and hunger
for justice to all those who have bread. Amen.
FRENCH COMMUNITY OF THE ARK

We come to join in the banquet of love
Let it open our hearts and break down
    the fears
that keep us from loving each other.
DOMINICAN PRAYER

What God gives, and what we take,
'Tis a gift for Christ His sake;
Be the meal of beans and peas,
God be thank'd for those, and these.
Have we flesh, or have we fish,
All are fragments from His dish.
He His Church save, and the king,
And our peace here, like a spring,
Make it ever flourishing.

ROBERT HERRICK (1591–1674)

Most gracious God, who has given us Christ and with him all that is necessary to life and godliness: we thankfully take this our food as the gift of your bounty, procured by his merits. Bless it for the nourishment and strength of our frail bodies, to fit us for your cheerful service.

RICHARD BAXTER (1615–1691)

We give thanks, O God and Father, for the many mercies which you constantly bestow upon us. In supplying the food and drink necessary to sustain our present life, you show how much you care for our mortal bodies. And in supplying the life and the teachings of your Son, you reveal how much you love our immortal souls. Let the meal which we have enjoyed be a reminder to us of the eternal joy you promise to all who feed on your holy Word.

JOHN CALVIN (1509–1564)

Blessings for All People

Soften our hearts, O Lord, that we may be moved no less at the necessities and griefs of our neighbors, than if they concerned ourselves....Let us pity them as ourselves, and, in their adversity, let us have compassion upon them. Amen.

JOHANNES LUDOVICUS VIVES (1492–1540)

Almighty God, the fountain of all wisdom, you know our necessities before we ask and our ignorance in asking: Have compassion on our weakness, and mercifully give us those things which for our unworthiness we dare not, and for our blindness we cannot ask; through the worthiness of your Son, Jesus Christ our Lord, who lives and reigns with you and the Holy Spirit, one God, now and for ever. Amen.

THE BOOK OF COMMON PRAYER

Do all the good you can,
In all the ways you can,
In all the places you can,
At all the times you can,
To all the people you can,
As long as you ever can.

JOHN WESLEY (1703–1791)

How should one live?
Live...
welcoming
to all.

MECHTILD OF MAGDEBURG (1210?–1282)

Eternal Spirit...
Source of all that is and that shall be...
Loving God, in whom is heaven:
The hallowing of your name echo
    through the universe!
The way of your justice be followed
    by the peoples
    of the world!
Your heavenly will be done
    by all created beings!
Your commonwealth of peace and freedom
    sustain our hope and come on earth.
With the bread we need for today, feed us.
In the hurts we absorb from one another,
    forgive us.
In times of temptation and test, strengthen us.
From trials too great to endure, spare us.
From the grip of all that is evil, free us.
For your reign in the glory of the power
    that is love,
    now and for ever. Amen.

A NEW ZEALAND PRAYER BOOK

Surrender your rights
    to another,
  surrender your rights
    to the other
  whether friend or foe,
    let them go,
  Christ is always
    the other.

ESTHER DE WAAL

———

Let my mind look unto you
in all its searchings, shinings, certitudes.
Let my body work for you
with its full health and abilities.
Let your love pass
into the depth of my heart,
into the heart of my prayer,
into the heart of my whole being;
so that I desert myself
and dwell and move in you
in peace, now and evermore.

ERIC MILNER-WHITE (1884–1963)

More things are wrought by prayer
Than this world dreams of.
Wherefore let thy voice
Rise like a fountain for me night and day.
For what are men better than sheep or goats,
That nourish a blind life within the brain,
If knowing God, they lift not hands of prayer,
Both for themselves, and for those who call
    them friend.
For so the whole round earth is every way
Bound by gold chains about the feet of God.
ALFRED LORD TENNYSON (1809–1892)

Let me be at peace within myself.
Let me accept that I am profoundly loved
    and need never be afraid.
Let me be aware of the source of being
    that is common to us all
    and to all living creatures.
Let me be filled with the presence
    of the great compassion
    toward ourselves and toward all
    living beings.
Realizing that we are all nourished
    from the same source of life,

may I so live that others not be deprived
of air, food, water, shelter, or the chance
to live.
Let me pray that I myself cease to be
a cause of suffering to others.
With humility let me pray for the
establishment
of peace in our hearts and on earth.
May God kindle in me
the fire of love
to bring me alive
and give warmth to the world.
Lead me from death to life,
from falsehood to truth;
lead me from despair to hope,
from fear to trust;
lead me from hate to love,
from war to peace.
Let peace fill my heart,
the world, the universe.

A NEW ZEALAND PRAYER BOOK, ADAPTED

Love the earth and the animals,
   despise riches,
   give alms to everyone who asks,
Stand up for the stupid and crazy,
   devote your income and labor
   to others,
Hate tyrants and argue not concerning God.

WALT WHITMAN (1819–1892)

———

O Jesus, Son of the living God, who became man and made the supreme sacrifice of yourself in order to reveal the mystery of the Father's love and his plan of mercy and salvation for all peoples, we adore you and praise you, because you have enlightened and redeemed us.

O Jesus, you who sent out your apostles to gather in the harvest from all the fields of the world and did promise to draw all men to yourself on the Cross, we thank you for having sent to us those who have taught us the truth and made us sharers in your grace.

POPE JOHN XXIII (1881–1963)

You Lord, alone, are all Your children need
And there is none beside;
From You the streams of blessedness proceed;
In You the blessed abide,
Fountain of life and all-abounding grace,
Our source, our center and our
    dwelling place!
MADAME GUYON (1648–1717)

As we really love God, we shall strive to render Him this service, by promoting His Glory in all we do—not in great things only, but in trifles too; and furthermore we shall strive earnestly to lead our neighbor to love and serve Him too so that He may everywhere and in all things receive glory and honor. As we really love our neighbor, we shall rejoice in all that he possesses that is good, so far as he turns it to God's glory; we shall gladly render him every service which he can require at our hands; we shall be zealous for his soul's welfare, and seek to promote it as our own, because it is acceptable to God. This is true charity, real solid love of God for His own sake, and of man for God's sake.
SAINT FRANCIS DE SALES (1567–1622)

Blessed are they who have the gift of making friends, for it is one of God's best gifts. It involves many things, but above all, the power of going out of one's self, and appreciating whatever is noble and loving in another.

THOMAS HUGHES

How brief is our span of life compared with the time since you created the universe. How tiny we are compared with the enormity of your universe. How trivial are our concerns compared with the complexity of your universe. How stupid we are compared with the genius of your creation. Yet during every minute and every second of our lives you are present, within and around us. You give your whole and undivided attention to each and every one of us. Our concerns are your concerns. And you are infinitely patient with our stupidity. I thank you with all my heart—knowing that my thanks are worthless compared with your greatness.

FULBERT OF CHARTRES (C. 970–1028)

Lord, bind us to you and to our neighbor
  with love,
May our hearts not be turned away from you.
May our souls not be deceived
  nor our talents or minds
  enticed by allurements or error;
Thus may we love our neighbor as ourselves
  with strength,
  wisdom, and gentleness.
With your help, you who are blessed throughout all ages.

SAINT ANTHONY OF PADUA (1190?–1231)

———

May you laugh often and much; win the respect of intelligent people and the affection of
children; earn the appreciation of honest crit-
ics and endure the betrayal of false friends; ap-
preciate beauty, and find the best in others; leave
the world a bit better, whether by a healthy child,
a garden, or a redeemed social condition. To
know even one life has breathed easier because
you have lived...this is to have succeeded.

You who are the true sun of the world, rising and never going down, who by your most wholesome appearing and sight nourishes and makes joyful all things in heaven and on earth; we beseech you mercifully and favorably to shine in our hearts, that the night and darkness of sin, and the mists of error on every side being driven away, and with you shining in our hearts, we may all our life long go without any stumbling or offense, and may walk as in the daytime, being pure and clean from the works of darkness; and abounding in all good works which you have prepared for us to walk in.

DESIDERIUS ERASMUS (1466?–1536)

Help me now to be quiet, relaxed and receptive, accepting the thought of your healing grace at work, deep within my nature.

LESLIE D. WEATHERHEAD (1893–1976)

*T*each me to seek you, and reveal yourself to me when I seek you, for I cannot seek you except you teach me, nor find you, except you reveal yourself.

SAINT ANSELM OF CANTERBURY (1033–1109)

---

*S*trengthen my personality.
Enlighten my inner search.
Prevent the self-centeredness of
    excessive scrupulousness.
Point me back to life.
Shake me out of my indifference.
Shake me out of my satisfaction with
    partial righteousness.
Shake me until I see the need for right
    to prevail
wherever life exists.

REX CHAPMAN

When the sins in my soul are increasing, I lose the taste for virtuous things. Yet even at such moments, Lord, I know I am failing you—and failing myself. You alone can restore my taste for virtue. There are so many false friends willing to encourage sin. But your friendship alone can give the strength of mind to resist and defeat sin.

SAINT TERESA OF ÁVILA (1515–1582)

Blessings on Work

God, our Father, we are exceedingly frail and indisposed to every virtuous and gallant undertaking. Strengthen our weakness, we beseech you, that we may do valiantly in this spiritual war; help us against our own negligence and cowardice, and defend us from the treachery of our unfaithful hearts; for Jesus Christ's sake. Amen.

THOMAS À KEMPIS (1380–1471)

We give You thanks for our work, and for the health to do it. We thank You for skill of hand, for accuracy of eye and mind and brain, to earn a living and to do the work of a house and home. We thank You for the friends and the comrades whom You have given to us, for those in whose company joys are doubly dear, and in whose presence sorrow's pain is soothed.

WILLIAM BARCLAY

Let us work as if success depended upon ourselves alone; but with heartfelt conviction that we are doing nothing and God everything.

SAINT IGNATIUS LOYOLA (1491–1556)

Keep us, Lord, so awake in the duties of our calling that we may sleep in Your peace and wake in Your glory.

JOHN DONNE (1573–1631)

Lord, You put me in the world for something; show me what it is. Help me to work out Your purpose for my life. I cannot do much, but like the widow who gave out of her poverty, I cast my time and eternity in Your treasury (Mark 12:44). I am all Yours. Take me. Enable me to glorify You in everything I do, in everything I say, and with everything I have. Amen.

CHARLES SPURGEON (1834–1892)

May there always be work for your
    hands to do.
May your purse always hold a coin or two.
May the sun always shine upon your
    window pane.
May a rainbow be certain to follow each rain.
May the hand of a friend always be near
    to you, and
May God fill your heart with gladness
    to cheer you.

TRADITIONAL IRISH BLESSING

O Lord, support us all the day long, until the shadows lengthen and the evening comes, and the busy world is hushed, and the fever of life is over, and our work is done. Then in your mercy grant us a safe lodging, and a holy rest, and peace at the last.

JOHN HENRY NEWMAN (1801–1890)

———

Lord, as we begin our work this day, give us a freshness of spirit, a lightness of movement, and a swiftness to do good. We ask for patience when everything does not fall neatly into place; when tasks take longer than we had planned; when interruptions threaten our hoped-for schedules. Let us remember that all of our actions begin, go forward, and end in you; and that without you we have no strength, no power, no will, to do anything at all. We pray and commit our day to you, for the sake of Jesus' own work and love for us. Amen.

ISABEL ANDERS (1997)

O Eternal God, who has created me to do the work of God after the manner of men, give me Your grace that I may be a prudent spender of my time, so that I may be profitable to the Christian commonwealth; and by discharging all my duty, may glorify You.

JEREMY TAYLOR (1613–1667)

Give me, dear Lord, a pure heart and a wise mind, that I may carry out my work according to your will. Save me from all false desires, from pride, greed, envy, and anger, and let me accept joyfully every task you set before me. Let me seek to serve the poor, the sad and those unable to work. Help me to discern honestly my own gifts that I may do the things of which I am capable, and happily and humbly leave the rest to others. Above all, remind me constantly that I have nothing except what you give me, and can do nothing except what you enable me to do.

JACOB BOEHME (1575–1624)

The outward work will never be puny if the inward work is great. And the outward work can never be great or even good if the inward one is puny or of little worth. The inward work invariably includes in itself all expansiveness, all breadth, all length, all depth. Such a work receives and draws all its being from nowhere else except from and in the heart of God. To God be the glory.

MEISTER ECKHART (1260?–1327?), ADAPTED

———

My God, you are always close to me. In obedience to you, I must now apply myself to outward things. Yet, as I do so, I pray that you will give me the grace of your presence. And to this end I ask that you will assist my work, receive its fruits as an offering to you, and all the while direct all my affections to you.

BROTHER LAWRENCE (1611–1691)

Dearest Lord, teach me to be generous.
Teach me to serve You as You deserve;
To give and not to count the cost;
To fight and not to heed the wounds;
To toil and not to seek for reward,
Save that of knowing that
I do Your will, O God.

SAINT IGNATIUS OF LOYOLA (1491–1556)

Part II

Occasional
Blessings

Blessings in the Event of Disagreements

Let us look at our own shortcomings and leave other people's alone; for those who live carefully ordered lives are apt to be shocked at everything, and we might well learn very important lessons from the persons who shock us.

SAINT TERESA OF ÁVILA (1515–1582)

O God, you have bound us together in a common life. Help us, in the midst of our differences, to confront one another without hatred or bitterness, and to learn always to work together with mutual forbearance and respect, through Jesus Christ our Lord. Amen.

Let peace abound in our small company. Purge out of every heart the lurking grudge. Give us grace and strength to forbear and to persevere. Offenders ourselves, give us the grace to accept and to forgive offenders. Forgetful, help us to bear cheerfully the forgetfulness of others. Give us courage and gaiety and the quiet mind.

Almighty and tender Lord Jesus Christ,
Just as I have asked you to love my friends
So I ask the same for my enemies.
You alone, Lord, are mighty.
You alone are merciful.
Whatever you make me desire for my enemies,
Give it to them.
And then give the same back to me.
If I ever ask for them anything
Which is outside your perfect rule of love,
Whether through weakness, ignorance,
    or malice,
Good Lord, do not give it to them
And do not give it back to me.
You who are the true light, lighten their darkness.
You who are the whole truth, correct
    their errors.
You who are the Incarnate Word,
    give life to their souls.
Tender Lord Jesus,
Let me not be a stumbling block to them
Nor a rock of offense.
My sin is sufficient to me,
    without harming others.
I, a slave to sin,
Beg your mercy on my fellow slaves.

Let them be reconciled with you,
And through you reconciled to me.

SAINT ANSELM OF CANTERBURY
(C. 1033–1109)

———

Where there is charity and wisdom,
there is neither fear nor ignorance.
Where there is patience and humility,
there is neither anger nor vexation.
Where there is poverty and joy,
There is neither greed nor avarice.
Where there is peace and meditation,
there is neither anxiety nor doubt.

SAINT FRANCIS OF ASSISI (1182–1226)

———

Blessings on the Earth and Natural Things

As often as you can, take a trip out to the fields to pray. All the grasses will join you. They will enter your prayers and give you strength to sing praises to God.

RABBI NACHMAN OF BRESLOV

Mighty One, in the woods I am blessed. Happy is everyone in the woods. Every tree speaks through You. O God! What glory in the woodland! On the heights is peace—peace to serve Him.

LUDWIG VAN BEETHOVEN (1770–1827)

Blessings for Pets and Other Creatures

O Supreme Spirit of Creation,
  from Your sacred breath came forth
  birds and beasts, fish and fowl,
  creatures of such variety and beauty
  that we are continuously amazed
  at Your divine imagination.
These children of Yours
  have been blessed by You, their Creator,
  with simplicity, beauty and a cosmic
  purpose.

They have been blessed as well
    by our greatest grandfather, Adam,
    who in Edenland gifted each with its
    own name.
They have also been blessed with protection
    by our ancient ancestor Noah,
    patron saint of those
    who seek to preserve all that You
    have created.
Sheep and goats, donkeys and cows,
    doves and serpents, fish and birds of the air
    were blessed by Jesus, Your Son,
    by His being born in their company
    and by His making use of them in
    His teachings.

May we, in this holy pattern, now bless _____ ,
    by taking delight in his/her beauty and
    naturalness.
May we bless this animal
    with a Noah-like protection
    from all that might harm him/her.
May we, like Adam and Eve,
    speak to this creature of Yours
    with kindness and affection,
    reverencing his/her life and purpose
    in our communal creation.

May we never treat this creature as a
    dumb animal,
      but rather let us seek to learn its language
      and to be a student of all the secrets
      that it knows.

May Your abundant blessing rest upon
    this creature
      who will be a companion for us in the
      journey of life.
Amen.

EDWARD HAYS

We beseech You, O Lord,
to hear our supplication
on behalf of the whole creation,
who after their kind, bless, praise,
and magnify You forever.
Grant that all cruelty may
cease out of our land and deepen
our thankfulness to You for the
faithful companionship of
those whom we delight to call
our friends.

ROYAL SOCIETY FOR THE PREVENTION OF
CRUELTY TO ANIMALS, ADAPTED

*I*t was quite incomprehensible to me—this was before I began going to school—why in my evening prayers I should pray for human beings only. So when my mother had prayed with me and had kissed me good night, I used to add silently a prayer that I had composed myself for all living creatures. It ran thus:

O heavenly Father, protect and bless all things that have breath; guard them from all evil and let them sleep in peace.

ALBERT SCHWEITZER (1875–1965)

Blessings for Those Who Perform Manual Labor

*B*less today the depressed rural world, the worker who, with his sweat, also waters his affliction, and who cannot wait any longer for full and effective recognition of his dignity, which is not inferior to that of any other member of society.

POPE JOHN PAUL II, ADDRESS TO INDIANS AND PEASANTS AT CUILAPA, MEXICO, 1979, ADAPTED

We bless you, Lord,
For the dignity of human work.
We bless you, Lord,
For the right to work.
Let us go forth in peace and joy.
Thanks be to God!

THOMAS G. SIMONS

———

Humbly, simply, we come early, praise God's
kindness, his great mercy. Beg him pity our distress, grant forgiveness for each trespass. Bitter
each day is our labor. As we worship in this
temple, fill our souls with his great peace. Now
we know God's grace will never cease. Sometimes we bear pain and suffering till our hearts
are full of darkness. Father, never from us depart, keep us poor folk in your kind heart. God,
give grace to us and gladness, bring us joy despite our sadness. May your mercy be our stay,
may your love enlighten each day.

CHAO TZU-CH'EN, CHINA

Dear Lord, bless those who perform manual labor, who choose voluntary poverty, and who do works of mercy. Besides inducing cooperation, besides overcoming barriers and establishing the spirit of brotherhood (besides just getting things done), manual labor enables us to use our body as well as our hands....Our bodies are made to be used, just as they are made to be respected as temples of the soul. God took on human flesh and became man. He shared our human nature. We believe in the resurrection of the body, free from fatigues, free from pain and disease and distortions and deformities, a glorified body, a body transfigured by love. Thus we respect and bless the body and those who perform manual labor, for using this gift well. Amen.

DOROTHY DAY (1897–1980), ADAPTED

Blessings for
the Unemployed

Heavenly Father, we remember before you those who suffer want and anxiety from lack of work. Guide the people of this land so to use our public and private wealth that all who seek employment may find suitable and fulfilling work, and receive just payment for their labor; through Jesus Christ our Lord. Amen.

I've lost my job. I know that it isn't my fault, God, but I feel as if it were. And I'm frightened. Will I be able to find another job? All the securities and responsibilities of my life are threatened. Help me, God. Help me to know who I am and what I can do, and to speak and act with such confidence in that knowledge that a new way will open for me.

AVERY BROOKE

Blessings on the Whole of Our Lives

Dear Lord, help me to spread Your fragrance
   everywhere I go.
Flood my soul with Your spirit and life.
Penetrate and possess my whole being
   so utterly
that all my life may only be a
   radiance of Yours.
Shine through me, and be so in me that
   every soul I come in contact with
   may feel Your presence in my soul.
Let them look up and see no longer me
   but only You, O Lord!

JOHN HENRY NEWMAN (1801–1890)

————

Lord, my thoughts turn in upon myself. Turn them upward to you and outward to your other children, that I may forget myself, and lose all fear and anxiety, all self-seeking and self-consciousness, in worship of you and in love of others. O save me from myself to worship, love and serve in perfect freedom.

GEORGE APPLETON

How should Our Lord fail to grant His graces to him who asks for them from his heart when He confers so many blessings even on those who do not call on Him? Ah, He would not so urge and almost force us to pray to Him if He had not a most eager desire to bestow His graces on us.

SAINT JOHN CHRYSOSTOM (347?–407)

———

Lord, bind us to you and to our neighbor
      with love,
May our hearts not be turned away from you.
May our souls not be deceived
      nor our talents or minds
      enticed by allurements or error;
Thus may we love our neighbor as ourselves
      with strength,
      wisdom, and gentleness.
With your help, you who are blessed
      throughout all ages.

SAINT ANTHONY OF PADUA (1190?–1231)

Blessings on Sporting Activities

Let us learn in play, in playfulness before God to be something of a fool, not to take ourselves too seriously. In order to play, I have to forget myself. May the game absorb my attention so fully that I forget how I am feeling or who is watching me or how well I am playing. As with play, so with prayer. Give me self-forgetfulness; let me concentrate on God that I may find myself.

MURRAY BODO, O.F.M., ADAPTED

God of play, we thank you for the opportunity of athletics. We pray for your blessing on the [tryouts, start of a new season]. We ask your blessing on [participants/team members]. We thank you for strong, healthy bodies that enable us to play and compete. We ask you to help our team and our opponents to remain injury-free throughout the coming season. Help us to do our best. We ask this in the name of Jesus. Amen.

MITCH FINLEY, ADAPTED

At *the end of the season:* God of games and play, we thank you for the [name of sport] season that is coming to an end. We thank you for the efforts and enthusiasm of all the players, coaches, referees, and support personnel. Help us to recall this season as a time when both victory and defeat brought us closer to one another and to you. We pray in the name of Jesus, the Lord. Amen.

MITCH FINLEY

Blessings at the Beginning of a Journey

Blessed are You, Lord our God,
    for You have created a wide and
    wonderful world
    in which we can travel.
We ask Your blessing upon _____ ,
    as they are about to leave on a trip.
May You, Holy Guide of Travelers,
    be their ever-near companion,
    spreading the road before them
    with beauty and adventure.

Free that road from harm and evil,
    and send as their escorts
    Your holy spirits, Your angelic messengers,
    who accompanied the holy ones of
    days past....
May the blessing of the Father,
    and of the Son
    and of the Holy Spirit
    be upon you throughout this trip;
    may it shield you from all harm
    and bring you home again in safety
    and in peace. Amen.
EDWARD HAYS

O God, who did call Abraham to leave his home, and did protect him in all his wanderings, grant to those who now travel by land, sea, or air, a prosperous journey, a quiet time, and a safe arrival at their journey's end. Let the angel Raphael accompany them along your path of peace. Be to them a shadow in the heat, a refuge in storms, a protection in adversity, and grant that they may reach their destination and arrive safely back home, through Jesus Christ, our Lord. Amen.

PRIEST'S PRAYER BOOK

Blessings for the Responsible Discharge of Our Duties

Grant us, we beseech you, O Lord, to follow you wheresoever you go. In little daily duties to which you call us, bow down our wills to simple obedience, patience under pain or provocation, strict truthfulness of word or manner, humility and kindness. In great acts of duty or perfection, if you should call us to them, uplift us to sacrifice and heroic courage; that in all things, both small and great, we may be imitators of your dear Son, Jesus Christ our Lord.

CHRISTINA ROSSETTI (1830–1894)

Keep us, Lord, so awake in the duties of our calling that we may sleep in your peace and wake in your glory.

JOHN DONNE (1573–1631)

Lord Jesus,
I give you my hands to do your work.
I give you my feet to go your way.
I give you my eyes to see as you do.
I give you my tongue to speak your words.
I give you my mind that you may think in me.
I give you my spirit that you may pray in me.

Above all, I give you my heart that you may
    love in me your Father and all mankind.
I give you my whole self that you may grow
    in me, so that it is you, Lord Jesus
Who live and work and pray in me.

THE GRAIL PRAYER

If I have faltered more or less
In my great task of happiness;
If I have moved among my race
And shown no glorious morning face;
If beams from happy human eyes
Have moved me not; if morning skies,
Books, and my food, and summer rain
Knocked on my sullen heart in vain: —
Lord, thy most pointed pleasure take
And stab my spirit broad awake.

ROBERT LOUIS STEVENSON (1850–1894)

Blessings for Those on Vacation

Dear God, you who rested on the seventh day
and yet are still at work;
    in the course of this busy life
give us times of refreshment and relaxation
and grant that we may use our leisure
to rebuild our bodies and renew our minds.
We pray that our spirits may be opened
    continually
to the blessing and goodness of your creation.
Amen.

Summer has been a time for new adventures, for relaxing recreation and for informal learning. As we share what we have gained from this summer, let us remember that God our Father has given us minds and hearts to grow so that we can become fuller persons and thus more like his Son Jesus.

Thank you, God...for friends we visited or who visited us, sharing their life with us. For vacations and gardens, for ball games and bike riding, for swimming and suntans. For the sun and wind and rain, for lakes and mountains and prairies, for grass and flowers and trees and blue skies. Thank you, God!

THOMAS G. SIMONS, ADAPTED

Blessings on Meetings

Holy Spirit, you who create aliveness;
bless also this our gathering,
the speaker and the hearer;
fresh from the heart it shall come,
by your aid,
let it also go to the heart.

SØREN KIERKEGAARD (1813–1855)

God our Creator,
when you speak there is light and life,
when you act there is justice and love;
grant that your love may be present
in our meeting.
Grant that what we say and what we do
may be blessed. And fill us with your
Holy Spirit,
through Christ our Lord. Amen.

Blessings for Peace

May God the Father who made us bless us
May God the Son send his healing among us
May God the Holy Spirit move within us
and give us
eyes to see with, ears to hear with and hands
that your work might be done.
May we walk and preach the word of God
to all.
May the angel of peace watch over us,
and lead us at last by God's grace to
the Kingdom.

DOMINICAN BLESSING

I would like the angels of Heaven
    to be among us.
I would like an abundance of peace.
I would like full vessels of charity.
I would like rich treasures of mercy.
I would like cheerfulness to preside over all.
I would like Jesus to be present.
I would like the three Marys of illustrious
    renown to be with us.
I would like the friends of Heaven
    to be gathered around us
    from all parts.
I would like myself to be a rent payer to the Lord:
that if I should suffer distress,
    he would bestow a good blessing upon me.

    SAINT BRIGID OF IRELAND

———

*M*ay the peace of God, which passes all understanding, keep your hearts and minds in the knowledge and love of God, and of his Son Jesus Christ our Lord: and the blessing of God Almighty, the Father, the Son, and the Holy Ghost, be among you and remain with you always. Amen.

    THE BOOK OF COMMON PRAYER

May you have peace, a precious treasure to be sought out with great skill. Live your life that you may receive the blessings of the Lord. Then the peace of God our Father will be with you always.

Francis Paolo, adapted

Dear God,
We do not wish for the moon or stars.
All we want is peace.

Prayer faxed to
the Western Wall in Jerusalem

O Lord, giver of peace, make us peacemakers. Never let us aid and abet strife, or even unintentionally cause the least division among your people. Amen.

Charles Spurgeon (1834–1892)

Blessings for Those Undertaking New Ventures

Bless, O Lord, the beginning of this work, especially in the case of a young and tender thing; for that is the most important time when the character is being formed.

———

God, ever generous and caring in all our needs, we thank you and bless you for guiding us on the journey of life and lighting the path of unknown ways. May our hearts trust the way you have prepared and help us to be generous in sharing your goodness. Through Christ our Lord. Amen.

THOMAS G. SIMONS

———

Almighty God, who knows we are powerless to help ourselves, keep us in your care, body and soul. May we be kept from all bodily danger and preserved from evil thoughts; through Jesus Christ our Lord. Amen.

GREGORIAN SACRAMENTARY

When tiny fledgling birds launch away from the nest, or, as in the case of some birds, are pushed over the edge, they will find when they spread their wings that the *air* itself supports them. Is not God just like that supporting air? If God is utterly beneficent—and this I truly believe—then He is like a great river of loving purposefulness. We are to plunge in without trying to swim even with the current, let alone against it, and just keep our head above water, and face the way the river is going. If we utterly commit ourselves to His way and do our best, then the responsibility of our arrival at the goal of His purpose for us is His, not ours. Let us commit ourselves to Him..., for the real God is to be trusted, and whatever happens to us...we shall know that eternal Love still bears us on its bosom, and that we shall find our way home without regret.

LESLIE D. WEATHERHEAD (1893–1976)

*I*n the name of the merciful and
    compassionate God,
Praise belongs to God, the Lord of the worlds,
The merciful, the compassionate,
The ruler of the day of judgment!
You we serve and You we ask for aid.
Guide us in the right path.

THE KORAN

Blessing on the Creation of Works of Art

*L*iterature, painting, music—the most basic lesson that all art teaches us is to stop, look, and listen to life on this planet, including our own lives, as a vastly richer, deeper, more mysterious business than most of the time it ever occurs to us to suspect as we bumble along from day to day on automatic pilot. In a world that for the most part steers clear of the whole idea of holiness, art is one of the few places left where we can speak to each other of holy things.

FREDERICK BUECHNER

Blessing on Artists and Craftspeople

By what means did you make heaven and earth? What tool did you use for this vast work? You did not work as a human craftsman does, making one thing out of something else as his mind directs. These artists' minds can impose upon their materials whatever form they perceive within themselves by their inner eye. But how could their minds do this unless it was because you had made it? Bless, O Lord, all those who create in imitation of your most magnificent work.

Blessings on Church Musicians and Artists

O God, whom saints and angels delight to worship in heaven: Be ever present with your servants who seek through art and music to perfect the praises offered by your people on earth; and grant to them even now glimpses of your beauty, and make them worthy at length to behold it unveiled for evermore; through Jesus Christ our Lord. Amen.

THE BOOK OF COMMON PRAYER

———

Loving Creator
Watch over this work
and may it reflect the light of your presence.
May the effort of our human creations
    be as praise to you,
    and let our praise blend with the
joy of all creation.
Preserve us in your love
until we come to those eternal joys
which you promise in your love
through Jesus Christ our Lord.
Amen.

EVENING COLLECT, ADAPTED

Blessings on Business Endeavors

O Lord of the vineyard, we beg Your blessing upon all who truly desire to serve You by being diligent and faithful in their several callings, bearing their due share of the world's burden, and going about their daily tasks in all simplicity and uprightness of heart.

JOHN BAILLIE (1886–1960)

———

Jesus practiced what he preached. He said, "Turn the other cheek"; and in the Garden of Gethsemane, he healed the ear of the slave of the high priest who had come to arrest him. He said, "Love your enemies," and he forgave his executioners from the cross. In our daily work, then, give us the grace to act like Jesus. Let us be honest in our dealings with others, let us fulfill our mission of service and leadership with sincerity, and let us present ourselves to others humbly yet authentically, and let us go to our tasks nurtured by God's power.

HARRY A. OLSON, ADAPTED

Lord, help us in our work to put first things first, to do one thing at a time, and to learn the art of intense concentration. Give us, we pray, a balance of perception, organization, ability, and stamina, for your name's sake. Amen.

Blessings on Buildings and Construction

God our Father,
by the labor of men and women
you govern and guide
the work of building and constructing.
Hear the prayers of your people
and give to all who work on this [home/
    church/building]
an opportunity to create what enhances
    their human dignity
and draws them closer to each other
in the service of their brothers and sisters.
We ask this in Jesus' name. Amen.

Unless the Lord builds the house, its builders labor in vain" (Psalm 127:1). May the goodness of the Lord be on our efforts and may he bless the work of our hands with success in his eyes.

Blessings on Our Houses and Homes

I pray heaven to bestow
The best of blessings on
This house
and on all that shall hereafter
inhabit it.
May none but the honest and wise
Ever rule under this roof.

JOHN ADAMS (1735–1826), INSCRIPTION ON A MANTEL IN THE WHITE HOUSE

O eternal God, who alone makes a family
   to be of
   one mind in a home,
Help us, the members of this household,
   faithfully to
   fulfill our duties to you and to each other.
Put far from us all unkind thoughts, anger,
   and evil speaking.
Give us tender hearts, full of affection and
   sympathy toward all.
Grant us grace to feel the sorrows and trials
   of others
   as our own, and to bear patiently with
   their imperfections.
Preserve us from selfishness, and grant
   that, day by day,
   walking in love, we may grow up
   into the likeness
   of your blessed Son, and be found ready
   to meet him,
   and to enter with him into that place
   which he has gone to
   prepare for us;
For his sake, who lives and reigns with you
   and the Holy Ghost,
   one God, world without end.

*F*ather of all mankind, make the roof of my house wide enough for all opinions, oil the door of my house so it opens easily to friend and stranger, and set such a table in my house that my whole family may speak kindly and freely around it.

HAWAIIAN PRAYER

O God, make the door of this house wide enough to receive all who need human love and fellowship, and a heavenly Father's care; and narrow enough to shut out all envy, pride and hate.

Make its threshold smooth enough to be no stumbling-block to children, nor to straying feet, but rugged enough to turn back the tempter's power: make it a gateway to your eternal kingdom.

THOMAS KEN (1637–1711)

Gracious Lord,
These walls are precious to us
For they not only shut out
the cold and damp, the sun and heat
—they shelter our lives and guard our spirits.
From these doors we go out into the world
renewed and refreshed to live for You...
equipped and satisfied and enabled
to be your people in the world.

Blessed are you, O God,
for you framed the universe
as the dwelling-place of your glory
and your Word pitched a tent in our midst.
Grant that those who dwell in this place
may find only harmony and peace.
May they, and all who search for you,
find shelter in your presence.
This we ask through Jesus Christ our Lord.
Amen.

OCCASIONAL CELEBRATIONS, ANGLICAN
CHURCH OF CANADA

Except the Lord build the house,
their labor is but lost that build it.
Encircle this dwelling place with your
    protection, O God;
may your holy angels encompass these walls,
and peace be within them.
Open the windows and doors of this house that
the light and love of your Holy Spirit may
    shine within,
a light in the world for warmth and welcome.
In the name of God,
peace to this house,
peace to this place.
God make it a haven for all who live here.

A NEW ZEALAND PRAYER BOOK

Blessed is the spot, and the house,
    and the place, and the city,
        and the heart, and the mountain,
and the refuge, and the cave,
    and the valley, and the land,
        and the sea, and the island,
    and the meadow where mention
        of God has been made,
        and his praise glorified.

BAHA'I PRAYER BY BAHA 'U' LLA'H

Blessings at the Start of a School Year

Dear Lord Jesus, on this first day of school, please help us through the confusion and new-ness. We wish for comfort and happiness dur-ing the day. Help us to succeed and have others succeed. We ask for your strength to guide us, your love to help us, and your wisdom to pull us through.

EMILIE CHANDLER (1997)

We sit at Jesus' feet and earnestly pray for His blessed aid to make our dull minds grow brighter, and our feeble understanding able to receive knowledge. Amen.

CHARLES SPURGEON (1834–1892), ADAPTED

Blessing on New Students

God, our loving Father, we ask you to bless our new students and help them to feel wel-come and a part of our school community. Re-

mind students and teachers who are "old tim-
ers" to be helpful and courteous to our new students. At the same time, help our newcomers
to find their way around and adapt to their new
classes easily. Bless them with many friends and
much success in all that they do. We pray in the
name of Jesus, the Lord. Amen.

MITCH FINLEY

Blessings for Teachers

God our creator, we pray for all who teach
in church or in school. Give them honesty,
sincerity, and a concern for their students
that will help convey the lessons that they
teach.

Bless the books and the tools used by teachers
and students, so that they become a source
of learning and exploration.

Help teachers and students create a healthy
learning climate so all can have the freedom to learn. Guide all of us out of dark
confusion and into the light of wisdom, for
in you is all wisdom. Amen.

Let every teacher be a stranger to the desire for domination, vainglory, and pride; one should not be able to fool him by flattery, nor blind him by gifts, nor conquer him by the stomach, nor dominate him by anger; but he should be patient, gentle, and humble as far as possible; he must be tested and without partisanship, full of concern, a lover of souls.

ANONYMOUS DESERT FATHER

Blessings on Our Studies

O Lord, who is the fountain of all wisdom and learning, you have given me the years of my youth to learn the arts and skills necessary for an honest and holy life. Enlighten my mind, that I may acquire knowledge. Strengthen my memory that I may retain what I have learned. Govern my heart, that I may always be eager and diligent in my studies. And let your Spirit of truth, judgment, and prudence guide my understanding, that I may perceive how everything I learn fits into your holy plan for the world.

JOHN CALVIN (1509–1564)

Take, Lord, and receive all my freedom, my memory, my intelligence and my will—all that I have and possess. You, Lord, have given those things to me. I now give them back to you, Lord. All belongs to you. Dispose of these gifts according to your will. I ask only for your love and your grace, for they are enough for me.

SAINT IGNATIUS OF LOYOLA (1491–1556)

God help my thoughts! They stray from me, setting off on the wildest journeys. When I am in church, they run off like naughty children, quarreling, making trouble. When I read the Bible, they fly to a distant city....My thoughts can cross an ocean with a single leap; they can fly from earth to heaven, and back again, in a single second. They come to me for a fleeting moment, and then away they flee....They slip from my grasp like tails of eels; they swoop hither and thither like swallows in flight. Dear, chaste Christ, who can see into every heart and read every mind, take hold of my thoughts. Bring my thoughts back to me, and clasp me to yourself.

CELTIC SCHOLAR'S PRAYER

Blessings on the Study of Scriptures

May your Spirit, O Christ, lead me in the right way, keeping me safe from all forces of evil and destruction. And, free from all malice, may I search diligently in your Holy Word to discover with the eyes of my mind your commandments. Finally, give me the strength of will to put those commandments into practice through all the days of my life.

THE VENERABLE BEDE (672?–735)

Lord, as I read the Psalms, let me hear you singing. As I read your words, let me hear you speaking. As I reflect on each page, let me see your image. And as I seek to put your precepts into practice, let my heart be filled with joy.

SAINT GREGORY OF NAZIANZUS (329?–390)

Lord let the words of Scripture be carefully taken in and stored up in the recesses of my soul and stamped with the seal of silence; afterwards may they be brought forth from the jar of your heart with great fragrance; like some perennial fountain, may they flow abundantly from the veins of experience and irrigating channels of virtue and pour forth copious streams as if from some deep well in your heart.

ABBA NESTEROS

Blessing at the Beginning of Holiday Activities

(Christmas baking, gift shopping)

Lord, as we begin this whole routine
    all over again
When we find that our wish-list exceeds
    our income
And we run out of stamps for holiday cards
And get tangled in the ribbons and string
Of festive decorations...
And stuck to the tape of package
    wrappings—

Remind us of what it is all about:
Celebrating your love.
Bless our efforts to cheer each other
Despite the weather and the stress and
    the crowds.
Let the works of our hands and the carols
    in our hearts
be as prayers to you in the midst of our busy
    holiday activities.
Give us joy and peace—the gifts we need
    most of all,
For the sake of your Son, our Savior. Amen.
ISABEL ANDERS (1997)

Blessings for Hospitality and Welcome

As the fire under the stone floor
of my dwelling place burns brightly to
    warm my house
So may the love of God warm my heart
and the hearts of those who step
    over my threshold.
FORMOSAN PRAYER

I saw a stranger yestre'en
Put food in the eating place
Drink in the drinking place
Music in the listening place.
And in the sacred name of the Triune God
He blessed myself and my house,
My cattle and my dear ones.
And the lark sang in her song,
    Often, often, often,
Goes the Christ in stranger's guise,
    Often, often, often,
Goes the Christ in stranger's guise.
    CELTIC PRAYER

———

*H*eaven,
we're told, is not unlike this,
the banquet celestial,
eternal convivium...
Yes! Around your table we
knew the Holy Spirit, come to bless
the food, the host, the hour, the willing guest.
    MADELEINE L'ENGLE

Part III

Blessings in
Good Times
and Bad

Blessings in
Times of Sorrow

Lord, come alive within my experience,
   within my sorrows and disappointment
   and doubts,
   within the ordinary movements of my life.
Come alive as the peace and joy and
   assurance that is
   stronger than the locked doors within,
   with which we try to shut out life.
REX CHAPMAN

O Lord, when I am bewildered and the world is all noise and confusion around me and I don't know which way to go and am frightened, then be with me. Put your hand on my shoulder and let your strength invade my weakness and your light burn the mist from my mind. Help me to move forward with faith in the way I should go.
AVERY BROOKE

Dear God, bless my sorrow and wash my eyes with tears until they can behold the invisible land where tears shall come no more.

HENRY WARD BEECHER (1813–1887), ADAPTED

Think not thou canst sigh a sigh,
And thy maker is not by;
Think not thou canst weep a tear,
And thy maker is not near.

O! he gives to us his joy
That our grief he may destroy;
Till our grief is fled and gone
He doth sit by us and moan.

WILLIAM BLAKE (1757–1827)

Receive poverty, want, sickness, and all miseries joyfully from the hand of God, and with equal joy receive consolation, refreshment, and all super-abundance. By this uniform joy in the will of God thou will deaden the stimulus of thy passions.

MACARIUS THE ELDER (300?–390)

What do you ask of us, O Christ? Above all to carry one another's burdens, and to entrust them to you in our prayer, which always remains poor.

You welcome all who come to you with their burdens, and it is as if, anytime, anywhere, you welcomed them into your house in Nazareth.

When we let ourselves be welcomed by you, the suffering Servant, the inward eye perceives, beyond our own confusion, a reflection of the Christ of glory, the Risen Lord.

And we are brought to life each time you visit us by the Holy Spirit, the Comforter.

BROTHER ROGER OF TAIZÉ

———

Lord our God, You know our sorrow better than we know it ourselves. You know how easily our fearful soul entangles itself with untimely and self-made cares. We pray to You: Let us clearly discern their inappropriateness and scorn them proudly, these busy self-made cares. But whatever care You do inflict upon us, let us receive it from Your hand with humility and give us the strength to bear it.

SØREN KIERKEGAARD (1813–1855)

Blessings in Times of Joy

I feel your gaze upon my heart this moment like the sunny silence of the morning upon the lonely field whose harvest is over. Some day I shall sing to you in the sunrise of some other world, "I have seen you before in the light of the earth, in the love of man." Let this be my last word, that I trust in your love.

RABINDRANATH TAGORE (1861–1941)

---

*Y*ou have struck our hearts with your love, and like arrows that stick in the heart, we bear your words in us.

SAINT AUGUSTINE (354–430)

---

*L*ord God, joy marks your presence; beauty, abundance, and peace are the tokens of your work in all creation. Work also in our lives, that by these signs we may see the splendor of your love and may praise you through Jesus Christ our Lord. Amen.

LUTHERAN LITURGY

You are a present joy, O Lord;
you will be ever our reward;
and great the light in you we see
to guide us to eternity.

THE VENERABLE BEDE (673–735)

This we owe God: We should know him, fear
him, worship him, love him, praise him, preach
and bless him, exalt him, glorify him, magnify
him, sanctify him, give thanks to him, submit
ourselves and all our things to him, be glorified through and take delight in him, rejoice in
him, trust in him and obey, and resign ourselves
to him.

DEVOTIO MODERNA (15TH CENTURY)

Blessings in Times of Suffering

Remember this: All suffering comes to an end.
And whatever you suffer authentically, God has
suffered it first.

MEISTER ECKHART (1260?–1327?)

God, where are you? What have I done to make you hide from me? Are you playing cat and mouse with me, or are your purposes larger than my perceptions? I feel alone, lost, forsaken.

You are the God who majors in revealing yourself. You showed yourself to Abraham, Isaac, and Jacob. When Moses wanted to know what you looked like, you obliged him. Why them and not me?

I am tired of praying. I am tired of asking. But I will keep on praying and asking and waiting because I have nowhere else to go. Jesus, you, too, knew the loneliness of the desert and the isolation of the cross. And it is through your forsaken prayer that I speak these words.

RICHARD FOSTER

Lord, grant us calm, if calm can set forth thee.
CHRISTINA ROSSETTI (1830–1894)

Lord, we pray not for tranquility; we pray that You grant us strength and grace to overcome adversity.
SAVONAROLA (1452–1498)

It is only when the apparent absurdity of life is faced in all truth that faith really becomes possible. Otherwise, faith tends to be a kind of diversion, a spiritual amusement in which one gathers up accepted, conventional formulas and arranges them in the approved mental patterns, without bothering to investigate their meaning, or asking if they have any practical consequences in one's life. Lord, grant us true faith.

THOMAS MERTON (1915–1968)

———

Your life, O Christ, is the power to stand,
rooted in compassionate courage
in the midst of and after the blow
 of any dark power.
O Good Lord, who compassionately endures
 all things
and saves us from the curse, glory to you!

THE SERVICE BOOK,
HOLY CATHOLIC APOSTOLIC CHURCH

Heavenly Father, assure us that yesterday's reverses have not broken us; that they have only given us added knowledge wherewith to grasp our problems more firmly; and that during the pause of the night, You have granted us new wisdom and strength. May Your presence in our hearts be our shield and buckler as we start the battle afresh. This day, be it of defeat or of victory—may it be Your day, O Lord. Create in us a stronger yearning for Your presence so that, chance what will, we shall draw closer unto You, learning to know You with a fuller knowledge and to love You with a deeper and deeper love. Amen.

BLESSING AND PRAISE:
A BOOK OF MEDITATIONS

Blessings for
Those Who Are Sick
and in Pain

Father, your Son accepted our sufferings to teach us the virtue of patience in human illness. Hear the prayers we offer for our sick brothers and sisters. May all who suffer pain, illness or disease realize that they are chosen to be saints, and know that they are joined in Christ in his sufferings for the salvation of the world.

Lord, teach me the art of patience while I am well, and give me the use of it when I am sick. In that day either lighten my burden or strengthen my back. Make me, who so often in health have discovered my weakness, to be strong in my sickness when I solely rely upon your assistance.

THOMAS FULLER (1608–1661)

We who stand in the world offer ourselves and our society for your blessed healing. We confess we have failed to love as you did. We have been socially unjust, and our society is imperfect, fragmented, and sometimes sick to death. Teach us your ways in the world and in this life which we share together....Lead us to worship you in the fullness of life as the Lord of politics, economics, and the arts. Give us light to seek true mortality, not in narrow legalisms but in sacrifice and open responsibility. Show us how to express our love for you in very specific, human service to others. Lord, change our hearts from hearts of stone to hearts of flesh, and let us give thanks to you for all of life.

MALCOLM BOYD

O Lord, holy Father, creator of the universe, author of its laws, you can bring the dead back to life, and heal those who are sick. We pray for our sick brothers and sisters that they may feel your hand upon them, renewing their bodies and refreshing their souls. Show to them the affection in which you hold all your creatures.

DIMMA, 7TH-CENTURY IRISH MONK

Dear Lord, you suffered so much pain in order to save me and all human beings from sin. Yet I find it hard to bear even this little pain in my body. Lord, because of your great pain, have mercy on my little pain. And if you wish me simply to bear the pain, send me the patience and the courage which I lack. It may seem strange to say it, but I would rather suffer the spiritual pain from the insults people hurl against me, in place of this physical pain. Indeed I enjoy spiritual pain suffered for your sake; and I happily embrace the disrespect of this world, so long as I am obeying your will. But in my feebleness, I cannot endure this present illness. Save me from it.

MARGERY KEMPE (C. 1373–1432)

Let him who would meet God visit the prison cell before going to the temple. Before he goes to church let him visit the hospital. Before he reads the Bible let him help the beggar at his door.

TOYOHIKO KAGAWA (1888–1960)

Christ, give me strength; your servant is not well.
The tongue that praised you is made silent,
Struck dumb by the pain of sickness.
I cannot bear not to sing your praises.
O, make me well again, make me whole,
That I may again proclaim your greatness.
Do not forsake me, I beseech you.
Let me return now to your service.

SAINT GREGORY OF NAZIANZUS (329?–390)

———

Dear Lord,
watch with those who wake or watch
    or weep tonight,
and give your angels charge over those
    who sleep;
tend your sick ones,
rest your afflicted ones, shield your joyous ones,
and all, for your love's sake.
God, we go into this night
confident that the dawn will break tomorrow;
grant that when we come to die,
we may go gladly and in hope,
confident in the resurrection.
Amen.

TRADITIONAL PRAYER

Dearest Lord, may I see you, today and every day, in the person of your sick, and while nursing them, minister unto you. Though you hide yourself behind the unattractive guise of the irritable, the exacting, the unreasonable, may I still recognize you and say, "Jesus, my patient, how sweet it is to serve you."

Lord, give me this seeing faith, then my work will never be monotonous. I will ever find joy in humoring the fancies and gratifying the wishes of all poor sufferers....

And, O God, while you are Jesus my patient, deign also to be to me a patient Jesus, bearing with my faults, looking only to my intention, which is to love and serve you in the person of each one of your sick. Amen.

DAILY PRAYER SAID BY
MOTHER TERESA'S WORKERS

Blessings in
Times of Trial

Lord, we acknowledge that the way ahead will not be easy. We will follow paths that we know may lead us into trial. Yet we are granted the grace and power which can make even our trials serve God's glory and bring about our own redemption. The cost of discipleship may be great. But following where the Lord leads—even if it puts us against the world—is the call to which we must give heed.

J. H. W. RHYS, ADAPTED

If You send evil upon us, it is in love. All the evils of the physical world are intended for the good of Your creatures, or are the unavoidable attendants on that good. And You turn that evil into good. You visit human beings with evil to bring them to repentance, to increase their virtue to gain for them greater good hereafter. Nothing is done in vain, but has its gracious end. You do indeed punish, yet even in wrath You remember mercy.

JOHN HENRY NEWMAN (1801–1890)

Who but you, Lord, could bring sweetness in the midst of bitterness, pleasure in the midst of torment? How wonderful are the wounds in my soul, since the deeper the wound, the greater is the joy of healing!

SAINT JOHN OF THE CROSS (1542–1591)

———

We shall match your capacity to inflict suffering by our capacity to endure suffering. We shall meet your physical force with soul force. Do to us what you will, and we shall continue to love you. We cannot in all good conscience obey your unjust laws, because non-cooperation with evil is as much a moral obligation as cooperation with good. Throw us in jail, and we shall still love you...but be ye assured that we will wear you down by our capacity to suffer. One day we shall win freedom, but not only for ourselves. We shall so appeal to your heart and conscience that we shall win you in the process, and our victory will be a double victory.

MARTIN LUTHER KING, JR. (1929–1968)

We bless God for our afflictions. We thank God for our changes. We extol God's name for loss of property. We feel that if God had not chastened us, we would have become too secure and self-confident. The path of trouble is the way home, Lord. Make this thought a pillow for my weary head. Amen.

Charles Spurgeon (1834–1892)

Blessings of Reconciliation

O God, be with us in this new day. Heal the wounds made by war and hatred. Ease the suspicions that lurk in the back of the mind about people we cannot see and do not know. Prepare us for a life as full of unexpected joys as it is of unexpected sorrows. All this we ask in Jesus' name—who is always the same—yesterday, today, and tomorrow.

Thai Christian Prayer

The hatred which divides nation from nation,
race from race, class from class,
Father, forgive.
The covetous desires of men and nations
to possess what is not theirs,
Father, forgive.
The greed which exploits the labors of men,
and lays waste the earth,
Father, forgive.
Our envy of the welfare and happiness
   of others,
Father, forgive.
Our indifference to the plight of the
homeless and the refugee,
Father, forgive.
The lust which uses for ignoble ends
the bodies of men and women,
Father, forgive.
The pride which leads to trust in ourselves
and not in God,
Father, forgive.

COVENTRY CATHEDRAL PRAYER, 1964

Lord, loose the cords of the mistakes
    that bind us,
as we release the strands we hold
    of others' guilt.
Lighten our load of secret debts
as we relieve others of their need to repay.
Forgive our hidden past with its
    secret shames
as we consistently forgive what others
    hide from us.

    MODERN PHRASING OF "THE LORD'S PRAYER"

He who approaches near to Me one span, I will approach to him one cubit; and he who approaches near to Me one cubit, I will approach near to him one fathom, and whoever approaches Me walking, I will come to him running, and he who meets Me with sins equivalent to the whole world, I will greet him with forgiveness equal to it.

    MISHKAT AL-MASABIH

Living Christ, you who were not minded
   to cling to eternal glory,
We open our minds to you.
Illumine them with your wisdom.
Make us one in understanding,
one in love,
one in soul,
one in spirit.
Help us to serve without pride or vanity
and to put others before ourselves.
May we not think of our concerns
without considering also the concerns
   of others.
In your name we pray. Amen.
   E. GLENN HINSON

A brother asked the abbot Pastor, "If I should
see my brother's fault, is it good to hide it?" The
old man said to him, "In what hour we do cover
up our brother's sins, God shall cover ours; in
what hour we do betray our brother's shames,
in like manner God shall betray our own."
   ANONYMOUS DESERT FATHER

Were we not forgiven, released from the consequences of what we have done, our capacity to act would be confined to one single deed from which we could never recover; we would remain victims of its consequences forever, not unlike the sorcerer's apprentice who lacked the magic formula to break the spell.

HANNAH ARENDT, ADAPTED

O Lord, bless all the people we love, at home and far away. Guide them by night and by day and keep them always under your loving care.

And, Lord, bless too the people we don't love as we should. Teach us to understand them and love them in spite of what we dislike about them. And help us to forgive those who have acted badly toward us and bless them, too.

AVERY BROOKE

If people must hate, let them hate suffering. If they must fight, let them fight injustice—till no one is poor and no one is despised and violence has vanished from our world.

RABINDRANATH TAGORE (1861–1941)

Dear Lord, You have made each person as unique and unrepeatable as a snowflake, allowing us to place our individual fingerprints upon this world and its life. We touch each other, and not always for good. We make mistakes, and we fail to understand one another. Yet we affirm Your goodness in creating us to be our very selves. We pray for the victory of peace, and for the more complex good that You can bring about through our differences. Reconcile us to Yourself, and to each other, we pray. Amen.

ISABEL ANDERS (1997)

Let us love the poverty of others as Jesus loves it. Let us see them with the eyes of His own compassion. But we cannot have true compassion on others unless we are willing to accept pity and receive forgiveness for our own sins. Teach us what it means to be forgiven, that we may understand how to forgive. Then we will be glad that, in forgiving one another, we may act towards one another as He has acted towards us.

THOMAS MERTON (1915–1968)

*P*eace to all men of evil will. Let vengeance cease and punishment and retribution. The crimes have gone beyond measure; our minds can no longer take them in. There are too many martyrs. Lord, do not weigh their sufferings on your scales of justice. Pay them otherwise. Credit the torturers, the informers and traitors, with [the martyrs'] courage and strength of spirit, their dignity and endurance. Take all this into account, Lord, for the remission of the sins of their enemies, as the price of the triumph of justice. Take good and not evil into account. And let us remain in our enemies' thoughts not as their victims, not as a nightmare, but as those who helped them overcome their crimes. This is all we ask for them. Amen.

ANTHONY BLOOM,
PRAYER FROM A CONCENTRATION CAMP

Blessing in
Times of Transition

Lord God, in a constantly changing world we look to you as our rock of hope. Hear us as we pour out our hearts to you, and give us grace and secure protection; through your Son, Jesus Christ our Lord. Amen.

LUTHERAN LITURGY

———

Blessings in
Times of Silence and Retreat

As you find yourself in the rush and noise of life, may you have intervals where you may step within yourself and be still. May you wait upon God and feel his good presence as you carry through with your day's business.

WILLIAM PENN (1644–1718), ADAPTED

How seldom have long talks proved to be good and fruitful? Would not many if not most of the words we use be better left unspoken? We speak about the events of the world, but how often do we really change them for the better? We speak about people and their ways, but how often do our words do them or us any good? We speak about our ideas and feelings, as if everyone were interested in them, but how often do we really feel understood? We speak a good deal about God and religion, but how often does it bring us or others real insight? Words often leave us with a sense of inner defeat.

HENRI J. M. NOUWEN (1932–1996)

Loving God, look with mercy on your servants who seek in solitude and silence refreshment of soul and strengthening for service; grant them your abundant blessing in the peace of Christ our Lord.

THE EPISCOPAL DAILY OFFICE

O gracious and holy Father,
Give us wisdom to perceive you,
intelligence to understand you,
diligence to seek you,
patience to wait for you,
eyes to see you,
a heart to meditate on you,
and a life to proclaim you,
through the power of the spirit of Jesus Christ
our Lord.

SAINT BENEDICT (480?–547?)

Lord, may my desires change to your desires.
Lord, if a desire is good and profitable, give me
grace to fulfill it to your glory. But if it be hurtful and injurious to my soul's health, then re-
move it from my mind.

THOMAS À KEMPIS (1380–1471)

Come in this quiet moment of meditation; call me again, lead me in your way for me, let the assurance of your friendship take away my fears. Let every shadow make me look up into your blessed face. Let me rise up now and follow you.

LESLIE D. WEATHERHEAD (1893–1976)

Blessings on the Self

Temper my intemperance, O Lord,
O hallowed, O adored,
my heart's creator, mighty, wild,
temper thy untempered child.
Blaze my eye and blast my ear,
let me never fear to fear,
nor forget what I have heard,
even your voice, my Lord.
Even your Word.

MADELEINE L'ENGLE

Lord, give me the grace to use this world so as not to abuse it. Lord, grant that I may never go beyond or defraud my brother in any matter; for you are indeed the avenger of all.

THOMAS KEN (1637–1711)

Lord, love me passionately,
Love me often,
Love me long.
The more passionately you love me,
the more beautiful I become.
The more often you love me,
    the purer I become.
The longer you love me, the holier I become.

MECHTHILD OF MAGDEBURG (C. 1210–1280)

We pray for ourselves who live in peace and quietness that we may not regard our good fortune as proof of our virtue, or rest content to have our ease at the price of others' sorrow and tribulation.

REINHOLD NIEBUHR (1892–1971)

To reach satisfaction in all,
    desire its possession in nothing.
To come to possess all,
    desire the possession of nothing.
To arrive at being all,
    desire to be nothing.
To come to the knowledge of all,
    desire the knowledge of nothing.
SAINT JOHN OF THE CROSS (1542–1591)

My prayer is but a cold affair, Lord,
because my love burns with so small a flame.
But you who are so rich in mercy
will not mete out to them your gifts
according to the dullness of my zeal,
but as your kindness is above all human love
so let your eagerness to hear
be greater than the feeling in my prayers.
Do this for them and with them, Lord,
so that they may speed according to your will
and thus ruled and protected by you,
always and everywhere,
God through all ages. Amen.
SAINT ANSELM OF CANTERBURY (1033–1109)

God has created all things for good; all things for their greatest good; everything for its own good. What is the good of one is not the good of another; what makes one person happy would make another unhappy. God has determined, unless I interfere with His plan, that I should reach that which will be my greatest happiness. He looks on me individually. He calls me by my name. He knows what I can do, what I can best be, what is my greatest happiness, and He means to give it to me.

God knows what is my greatest happiness, but I do not. There is no rule about what is happy and good; what suits one would not suit another. And the ways by which perfection is reached vary very much; the medicines necessary for our souls are very different from each other. Thus God leads us by strange ways; we know He wills our happiness, but we neither know what our happiness is, nor the way. We are blind; left to ourselves we should take the wrong way. We must leave it to Him.

JOHN HENRY NEWMAN (1801–1890)

*I*t is Glory enough for me
That I should be Your servant.
It is grace enough for me
That You should be my Lord.

ARABIC PROVERB

———

*H*elp me, O God:
To desire eternal life with spiritual longing.
To keep death before my eyes daily.
To keep constant watch over my actions.
To remember that God sees me everywhere.
To call upon Christ for defense against
    evil thoughts
    that arise in my heart.
To guard my tongue against wicked speech.
To avoid much speaking.
To avoid idle talk.
Not to seek to appear clever.
To read only what is good to read.
To pray often.
To ask forgiveness daily for my sins,
and to seek ways to amend my life.
To obey my superiors in all things rightful.
Not to desire to be thought holy,
    but to seek holiness.

To fulfill the commandments of God
   by good works.
To love chastity,
To hate no one.
To avoid being jealous or envious of anyone.
Not to love strife.
Not to love pride.
To honor the aged.
To pray for my enemies.
To make peace after a quarrel,
   before the setting of the sun.
Never to despair of your mercy, O God of mercy.

SAINT BENEDICT (480?–547?)

———

Blessings for the Discernment of God's Will

1. I am a bow in your hands, Lord.
   Draw me, lest I rot.
2. Do not overdraw me, Lord, I shall break.
3. Overdraw me, Lord, and who cares
   if I break!

NIKOS KAZANTZAKIS, *REPORT TO GRECO*

Creator of the universe, infinite and glorious,
you give us laws to save us from our folly;
give us eyes to see your plan unfolding;
your purpose emerging as the world is made;
give us courage to follow the truth;
courage to go wherever you lead;
then we shall know blessings beyond
    our dreams;
then will your will be done. Amen.

A NEW ZEALAND PRAYER BOOK

Where I wander—You!
Where I ponder—You!
Only You, You again, always You!
You! You! You!
When I am gladdened—You!
When I am saddened—You!
Only You, You again, always You!
You! You! You!
In every trend, at every end,
Only You, You again, always You!
You! You! You!

MARTIN BUBER (1878–1965)

Almighty and eternal God, so draw our hearts to you, so guide our minds, so fill our imaginations, so control our wills, that we may be wholly yours, utterly dedicated to you; and then use us, we pray you, as you will, but always to your glory and the welfare of your people; through our Lord and Savior Jesus Christ. Amen.

ARCHBISHOP WILLIAM TEMPLE (1881–1944)

Our love of God, then, must not be gauged by the passing feelings we experience that are not controlled by the will, but rather we must judge them by the enduring quality of the will itself. For loving God means that we join our will to God's will. It means that our will consents to whatever the will of God commands. It means that we have only one reason for wishing anything, and the reason is that we know that God wills it.

SAINT AELRED OF RIEVAULX (1109–1167)

Lord Jesus, let me know myself;
Let me know you,
And desire nothing else but you.
Let me love myself only if I love you,
And do all things for your sake.
Let me humble myself and exalt you,
And think of nothing else but you.
Let me die to myself and live in you,
And take whatever happens as coming from you.
Let me forsake myself and walk after you,
And ever desire to follow you.
Let me flee from myself and turn to you,
So that I may merit to be defended by you.
Let me fear for myself, let me fear for you,
And be among those that are chosen by you.
Let me distrust myself and trust in you,
And ever obey for the love of you.
Look upon me that I may love you,
Call me, that I may see you,
And forever possess you, for all eternity.

SAINT AUGUSTINE (354–430)

Bless me in this life with but peace of my conscience, command of my affections, the love of Yourself and my dearest friends, and I shall be happy enough to pity Caesar.

SIR THOMAS BROWNE (1605–1682)

———

Someone has said that what we are is God's gift to us, and that what we become is our gift to God. It is true that God gives you and me the lumber of our lives, and offers to help us build from it a cathedral of love and praise. Give me the grace, O Lord, to make my person into a cathedral of enduring praise of you.

JOHN POWELL, S.J.

———

Maker of me, go on making me, and let me help You. Come, O Father, here I am: let us go on. I know that my words are those of a child, but it is Your child that prays to You. It is Your dark I walk in, it is Your hand I hold.

GEORGE MACDONALD (1824–1905)

Accustom yourself to the wonderful thought that God loves you with a tenderness, a generosity, and an intimacy which surpasses all your dreams. Give yourself up with joy to a loving confidence in God, and have courage to believe firmly that God's action toward you is a masterpiece of partiality and love. Rest tranquilly in this abiding conviction.

ABBE DE TOURVILLE

Grant us such grace that we may
  work Thy will,
And speak Thy words, and walk before
  Thy face,
Profound and calm like waters deep
  and still;
Grant us such grace.

CHRISTINA ROSSETTI (1830–1894)

Ah Jesus, sun of justice, make me clothe myself with you so that I may be able to live according to your will.

SAINT GERTRUDE OF HELFTA (1256?–1302?)

May you know the secret of joy—to no longer strive for your own way but commit yourself, easily and simply, to God's way, acquiesce to God's will, and in so doing find peace.

EVELYN UNDERHILL (1875–1941), ADAPTED

Grant me, O Lord, to know what I ought to know, to love what I ought to love, to praise what delights You most, to value what is precious in Your sight, to hate what is offensive to You. Do not suffer me to judge according to the sight of my eyes, nor to pass sentence according to the hearing of the ears of the ignorant; but to discern with a true judgment between things visible and spiritual, and above all things always to inquire what is the good pleasure of Your will.

THOMAS À KEMPIS (1380–1471)

Lord, bestow on me two gifts,
—to forget myself
—never to forget thee.
Keep me from self-love, self-pity, self-will
in every guise and disguise
nor ever let me measure myself by myself.
Save me from self,
my tempter, seducer, jailer;
corrupting desire at the spring,
closing the avenues of grace,
leading me down the streets of death.
Rather, let my soul devote to thee
its aspirations, affections, resolutions.

ERIC MILNER-WHITE (1884–1963)

Part IV

Blessings
in Community

Blessings on
the Family

Heavenly Father, you have given us a beautiful model of life in the Holy Family of Nazareth. Help us, O gracious Father, to create in our family another Nazareth where tenderness, love, understanding, and mutual respect abound. Amen.

MOTHER TERESA OF CALCUTTA (1910–1997)

Visit, we beseech thee, O Lord, our homes and drive far from them all the snares of the enemy: let your holy angels dwell therein to preserve us in peace; and may your blessing be upon us evermore; through Jesus Christ our Lord.

MARY BATCHELOR

Lord, behold our family here assembled.
We thank you for this place in which
   we dwell,
for the love that unites us,
for the peace accorded us this day,
for the hope with which we expect
   the morrow;
for the health, the work,
   the food and the bright skies
that make our lives delightful;
for our friends in all parts of the earth.
Give us courage and gaiety
   and the quiet mind.
Spare us to our friends,
   soften us to our enemies.
Bless us, if it may be,
   in all our innocent endeavors;
if it may not, give us the strength
to endure that which is to come
that we may be brave in peril,
constant in tribulation, temperate in wrath
and in all changes of fortune
and down to the gates of death,
loyal and loving to one another.
We beseech of you this help and mercy
for Christ's sake.

ROBERT LOUIS STEVENSON (1850–1894)

God bless our home, and help us to
   love each other true;
To make our home the kind of place
   where everything we do
Is filled with love and kindness,
A dwelling place for Thee,
And help us, God, each moment,
To live most helpfully.

———

For peace in every heart and home,
   we pray to you, Lord.
Lord, hear our prayer.
For those who feel alone,
   we pray to you, Lord.
Lord, hear our prayer.
For those who are sick or dying,
   we pray to you, Lord.
Lord, hear our prayer.
For us and for all your children,
   we pray to you, Lord.
Lord, hear our prayer.
For the kingdom, the power and the glory
   are yours, now and forever. Amen.
   TRADITIONAL FAMILY LITURGY

Praise Jesus in your home if not in the temple. Praise Him in the field if not in the market place. Praise Him with your family if not in the world. If you speak for God you will be refreshed, the saints will be encouraged, it will be useful to sinners, and the Savior will be honored.

CHARLES SPURGEON (1834–1892)

Blessings for Mercy and Compassion

All the wickedness in this world that man might work or think is no more to the mercy of God than a live coal in the sea.

WILLIAM LANGLAND (1330–1400),
THE BOOK CONCERNING PIERS THE PLOWMAN

Give me the grace, good Lord
To set the world at nought:
Of worldly substance, friends, liberty, life
and all,
to set the loss as nothing
for the winning of Christ.

SAINT THOMAS MORE (1478–1535)

Let us ask the Lord for mercy—
   God's forgiving love.
Let us thank the Lord for providence—
   God's caring love.
Let us bless the Lord for kindness—
   God's understanding love.
Let us praise the Lord for Christ's passion
   and death—God's proven love.
Let us thank the Lord for happiness—
   God's encouraging love.
Let us invoke the will of the Lord—
   God's unerring love.
And may we seek eternity—
   God's unending love.

———

Dear God,
We ask that you have mercy
on those who wish to oppress others
and that you protect the peacekeepers
involved in the peace and maintenance
of this world.
Give to these people the ability
to deal with those who continue to oppress
and give them the wisdom to show
   compassion
on all victims.

Most loving and gracious God,
I hear your words
in the laughter and tears of your people.
I touch your face
in those whom I see in my home,
    work, and church.
Help me to speak your words of life
in a world stained with sin.
Help me to give your compassionate,
    loving voice
sound in our world.
Help me, gentle and almighty God,
to be your voice,
your face,
your touch
in my world.
Help me to live your words of life.

Do not keep accounts with our Lord....Go bankrupt! Let our Lord love you without justice! Say frankly, "He loves me because I do not deserve it; that is the wonderful thing about Him; and that is why I, in my turn, love Him as well as I can without worrying....I know no other way of loving God." Therefore, burn your account books!

ABBE DE TOURVILLE

Blessings on the Future

Lord, may we see that nothing worth doing is completed in our lifetime; therefore, we must be saved by hope. Nothing true or beautiful or good makes complete sense in any context of history; therefore, we must be saved by faith. Nothing we do, however virtuous, can be accomplished alone; therefore we are saved by love. No virtuous act is quite as virtuous from the standpoint of our friend or foe as from our own standpoint. Therefore, we must be saved by the final form of love which is forgiveness. Amen.

REINHOLD NIEBUHR (1892–1971), ADAPTED

Thank you, God, that you have no need of the products of our busy activity, since you could give yourself everything without us. Thank you that the only thing that concerns you, that you desire intensely, is our faithful use of freedom and the preference we accord you over the things around us.

We acknowledge that the things that are given to us on earth are given purely as an exercise, a blank sheet on which we make our own mind and heart. We are a testing ground where you can judge whether we are capable of being translated to heaven and into your presence.

PIERRE TEILHARD DE CHARDIN (1881–1955)

Blessings for All Children

O God, whose beloved Son Jesus took children into his arms and blessed them: Give us grace to entrust these children to your never failing care and love, and bring us to your heavenly kingdom; through Jesus Christ our Lord, who lives and reigns with you and the Holy Spirit, one God, now and forever. Amen.

———

O Lord, shed the light of your love on my child. Keep him/her safe from all illness and injury. Enter this tiny one's soul and bring comfort with your peace and joy. Give this child the full measure of life on earth, and, in old age, let him/her die in the sure knowledge of your salvation. I do not ask that he/she be given wealth, power, or fame, but that he/she be poor in spirit, humble in action, and devout in your service. Dear Lord, smile upon my child and upon all others.

JOHANN STARCK (1680–1756), ADAPTED

Almighty God, heavenly Father, you have blessed us with the joy and care of children: Give us calm strength and patient wisdom as we bring them up, that we may teach them to love whatever is just and true and good, following the example of our Savior Jesus Christ. Amen.

THE BOOK OF COMMON PRAYER

Blessing for a Safe Birth

O gracious God, we give you humble and hearty thanks that you have preserved through the pain and anxiety of childbirth your servant _____ , who desires now to offer you her praises and thanksgivings. Grant, most merciful Father, that by your help she may live faithfully according to your will in this life, and finally partake of everlasting glory in the life to come; through Jesus Christ our Lord. Amen.

TRADITIONAL BLESSING

Blessings on New Parents

I pray the Father, Son, and Holy Ghost by the power He has given to fathers and mothers to bless their children that He will give you His benediction, and that He will detach you from earthly things and attach you to Himself. May you live as good Christians!

SAINT LOUISE DE MARILLAC (1591–1660)

———

Almighty God, giver of life and love, bless _____ and _____. Grant them wisdom and devotion in the ordering of their common life, that each may be to the other a strength in need, a counselor in perplexity, a comfort in sorrow, and a companion in joy. And so knit their wills together in your will and their spirits in your Spirit, that they may live together in love and peace all the days of their life; through Jesus Christ our Lord. Amen.

THE BOOK OF COMMON PRAYER

Dear friends: The birth of a child is a joyous and important occasion in the life of a family. It is also an occasion for rejoicing in the Christian community. I bid you, therefore, to join _____ and _____ in giving thanks to Almighty God our heavenly Father, the Lord of all life, for the gift of [child's name] to be their [son/daughter], and with [siblings' names] for a new [brother/sister]. Amen.

Blessings for Mothers

To Christ, our Mother in nature, our Mother in grace, who wanted altogether to become our Mother in all things, and who made the foundation of his work most humbly and most mildly in the maiden's womb....Our great God, the supreme wisdom of all things, arrayed and prepared himself in this humble place, all ready in our poor flesh, himself to do the service and the office of motherhood in everything. *Praise to the Mother of life and of all things.*

JULIAN OF NORWICH (C. 1342–AFTER 1413)

Lord, give me patience when wee hands tug at me with their small demands. Give me gentle and smiling eyes; keep my lips from hasty replies. Let not weariness, confusion, or noise obscure my vision of life's fleeting joys. So, when in years to come, my house is still—no bitter memories its rooms may fill. Amen.

A MOTHER'S PRAYER

Blessing for Fathers

Lord, bless our fathers
as they shelter and hold
support and encourage.
May their fatherly love be a
reflection of the strength of our
 Heavenly Father,
just as mothers reflect your nurturing love.
Keep them full of faith
toward their families.
Show them the way;
Guide them in the world;
And lead their steps toward home. Amen.

Blessings on Parents

O Lord God, whose will it is that, next to yourself, we should hold our parents in highest honor; it is not the least of our duties to beseech your goodness toward them. Preserve, we pray, our parents and home, in the love of your religion and in health of body and mind. Grant that through us no sorrow may befall them; and finally as they are kind to us, so may you be to them, O supreme Father of all.

DESIDERIUS ERASMUS (1466?–1536)

———

How I thank you, Father in Heaven, that you have preserved my earthly father [mother] here upon earth for a time such as this when I so greatly need him [her], a father [mother] who, as I hope, will with your help have greater joy in being my father [mother] the second time than he [she] had the first time in being so.

SØREN KIERKEGAARD (1813–1855)

Lord God, to come to you is to come home—
you who are the Eternal Father. From you every family derives its name, and every household
on earth finds its pattern in your love. Teach us
and help us, O Lord. Amen.

Blessings on the Elderly

When the signs of age begin to mark my body,
and still more when they touch my mind; when
the illness that is to diminish me or carry me
off strikes from without or is born within me;
when the painful moment comes in which I
suddenly awaken to the fact that I am ill or
growing old; in all those dark moments, O God,
grant that I may understand that it is you, provided only my faith is strong enough, who are
painfully parting the fibers of my being in order to penetrate to the very marrow of my substance and bear me away within myself.

PIERRE TEILHARD DE CHARDIN (1881–1955)

O God, who has in your love kept me vigorously and joyfully at work in days gone by, and does now send me joyful and contented into silence and inactivity; grant me to find happiness in you in all my solitary and quiet hours. In your strength, O God, I bid farewell to all. The past you know: I leave it at your feet. Grant me grace to respond to your divine call; to leave all that is dear on earth, and go alone to you. Behold, I come quickly, says the Lord. Come, Lord Jesus.

PRAYER OF AN INDIAN PRIEST IN OLD AGE

Grant us, O Lord, the royalty of inward happiness and the serenity which comes from living close to you. Daily renew in us the sense of joy and let the eternal spirit of the Father dwell in our souls and bodies, filling us with light and a grace so that, bearing about with us the infection of a good courage, we may be diffusers of life and may meet all ills and cross accidents with gallant and high-hearted happiness, giving thee thanks always for all things. Amen.

COMMITTEE ON AGING,
EPISCOPAL DIOCESE OF MARYLAND

O God of eternal love, you who give and sustain life in all its seasons, help us as we grow older to understand and affirm ourselves in our changing relationships with parents and others dear to us. Increase our sensitivity to their anxieties and frustrations. Give us thankful hearts for their love and nurture through the years. Grant us grace to forgive hurtful memories; and forgive us, Lord, for our unloving words and deeds. Calm our fears of loss and change, and open our hearts to the promise of new life in Jesus' name. Amen.

BARBARA BROWN

Blessings on Birthdays

O God, our times are in your hands: Look with favor, we pray, on your servant _____, as he/she begins another year. Grant that he/she may grow in wisdom and grace, and strengthen his/her trust in your goodness all the days of his/her life; through Jesus Christ our Lord. Amen.

THE BOOK OF COMMON PRAYER

Another year has passed, O Heavenly Father! We thank You that it was a time of grace, and we are not terrified by the thought that it was also a time for which we shall render an account; for we trust in Your mercy. The new year confronts us with its demands; and though we cannot enter upon it without humility and concern...yet we do not enter it altogether empty-handed. For You are ever the same Father without whose knowledge no sparrow falls to the ground. Amen.

SØREN KIERKEGAARD (1813–1855), ADAPTED

Watch over your child, O Lord, as his/her days increase; bless and guide him/her wherever he/she may be. Strengthen him/her when he/she stands; comfort him/her when discouraged or sorrowful; raise him/her up if he/she falls; and in his/her heart may your peace which passes understanding abide all the days of his/her life; through Jesus Christ our Lord. Amen.

Have you wept at anything
   during the past year?
Has your heart beat faster at the sight
   of young beauty?
Have you thought seriously about the fact
   that someday you are going to die?
More often than not do you really *listen* when
   people are speaking to you instead of just
   waiting for your turn to speak?
Is there anybody you know in whose place,
   if one of you had to suffer great pain,
   you would volunteer yourself?
If your answer to all or most of these
   questions is No, the chances are that
   you're dead.

FREDERICK BUECHNER

Blessings on
Wedding Anniversaries

O Lord, on this our wedding anniversary
we focus on the many blessings of
our years together:
The sharing of the cup of
sorrow and joy...
The blessings that have exceeded all hopes...
The oneness you have granted us in
earthly flesh...
That together we are more than the sum
of two persons...
That when we pray, our efforts are doubled...
And that you give us always the hope
of love multiplied further, in the years
    to come,
by your grace. Amen.

ISABEL ANDERS (1997)

Lord, today is our wedding anniversary.
Thank You for the exquisite gift of
   love fulfilled.
You have made our marriage what it was
   meant to be—
A dynamic demonstration of caring
   and sharing
Of giving and living.
When we invited You to our wedding
That day—did You plan our joy then—
Or did You wait until You moved in with us?

RUTH HARMS CALKIN

Blessing on Engagements

Dear God, today we make a beginning to-gether in love, in this place. Let [today] [or, this ring, if appropriate] be a reminder to us that the future flows from our commitment, our choice of each other. May all of our paths ahead be seen as connected to this special day, so that actions and goals and commitments to come later may all wind back to include love as we know it *right now*. Let us seek always to fit these new elements into what we already have, here, with each other—for mutual joy. This we ask in the name of Jesus our Lord. Amen.

Isabel Anders (1997)

Blessings on the Occasion of a Marriage

Blessed are you, Unnamable God, source of the universe, who created happiness and joy, bride and groom, gladness, exhilaration, pleasure and delight, love and friendship, harmony and peace. Unnamable God, may there soon be heard in the cities of Israel and in the streets of Jerusalem the sound of joy and the sound of happiness, the sound of Jew and Arab living in harmony, the sound of the bride and the sound of the groom, the jubilant sound of lovers joined under the wedding canopy, and of young people feasting and singing. Blessed are you, Unnamable God, who wish bride and groom to fill each other with joy.

Modern Jewish Wedding Blessing

Dear friends and family, we are gathered here in the presence of God to witness and to bless the covenant and commitment which _____ and _____ make this day with each other. Scripture tells us that we are created in God's image and love and that we are called to be vehicles of love unto each other. Our Savior Jesus Christ said to his disciples, "Love one another, as I have loved you." Fulfilling the two commandments for life that he gave us, to love God and our neighbor, we give praise and glory unto God and enrich the lives of one another. By the love we show unto others shall we be known as followers of Christ. God established a covenant relationship with us founded in love, mercy, forgiveness, and faithfulness. _____ and _____ come here today to commit their lives to a covenant union with each other, to live together faithfully, in love, forgiveness, and mercy. Therefore let us rejoice with them and pledge our love, friendship, and support unto them.

TRADITIONAL LITURGICAL BLESSING

O God, you have so consecrated the covenant of marriage that in it is represented the spiritual unity between Christ and his Church: Send therefore your blessing upon these your servants, that they may so love, honor, and cherish each other in faithfulness and patience, in wisdom and true godliness, that their home may be a haven of blessing and peace; through Jesus Christ our Lord, who with you and the Holy Spirit lives and reigns, one God, now and forever. Amen.

THE BOOK OF COMMON PRAYER

———

Blessings on Married Life

Lord, let not our marriage become stale and meaningless, a convenient shelter for married strangers. Let us, rather, seek and find ever new joy and wonder in each other, reliving the excitement of our early discovery of love together. Help us to make you the foundation of our marriage, the nuptial band that surrounds our love and keeps it sacred.

DOLORES CURRAN

I'm glad I'm married, Lord, but it isn't always easy. Help us then, Lord, to say what is on our hearts and minds in a way that the other can hear. And help each of us to listen.

Give me patience, Lord, when I should be patient and courage to speak out in disagreement when it is important. And remind me to do those little things which sometimes make all the difference.

AVERY BROOKE

Lord, we made a solemn promise: "For better or for worse." Today we are stumbling through "worse." Though our emotions are a bewildered mixture of agony and love, please quiet us, Lord. Free us from the desire to retaliate. Above all, help us both to remember we are as bound to our promise today as we were yesterday when we basked in the sunlight of "better."

Even now, dear Lord, help us to make it better again by not putting off what we both know we must eventually do if healing is to take place. The simple but beautiful word is *forgiveness*.

RUTH HARMS CALKIN

Keep us steadfast, O God, in the affections of our hearts that, in our constancy, we may forever be worthy of those who love and trust us.

HELENA T. OLTON

Blessings on a First Communion

As this soul approaches your Holy Supper for the first time, grant your protection, O Lord, strengthen it in faith, and prepare it for your way of love.

THE RACCOLTA, ADAPTED

May Jesus and Mary take your hand and lead the way as you come to the Holy Table for the first time. May you never lack for daily bread and drink. And may you always be fully fed on God's love and find its taste forever satisfying. May God in heaven bless you on this day and whenever you come to this Holy Table. Amen.

Lord, I acknowledge that I am far
  from worthy
To approach and touch this sacrament,
But I trust in that mercy
Which caused you to lay down your
  life for sinners,
That they might be saved from sin.
So I, a sinner, presume to receive these gifts.
Make me, O Lord, so to receive with lips
  and heart
And know by faith and by love,
That by virtue of this sacrament
I may die to sin as you died,
And rise to fullness of life as you rose.
May I be made worthy
To become a member of your holy body,
A stone in your living temple
And let me rejoice forever
In your eternal love.

SAINT ANSELM OF CANTERBURY (1033–1109),
PRAYER BEFORE RECEIVING COMMUNION

Blessings on Confirmation

Come, O Holy Spirit, and fill the heart of [person's name]. Make him/her strong in purpose, pure in heart, and always Christian in motive. Thank you for [name], whom you blessed in baptism, blessed again in first Eucharist, and now bless in confirmation. Fill all your people with joy, love, and your beloved Spirit.

DOLORES CURRAN

God of mercy and love,
new birth by water and the Spirit is your gift,
a gift none can take away;
grant that your servants may grow
into the fullness of the stature of Christ.
Fill them with the joy of your presence.
Increase in them the fruit of your Spirit:
the spirit of wisdom and understanding,
the spirit of love, patience, and gentleness,
the spirit of wonder and true holiness.
Amen.

A NEW ZEALAND PRAYER BOOK

O God our Father, let us find grace in your sight so as to have grace to serve you acceptably with reverence and godly fear; and further grace not to receive your grace in vain, nor to neglect it and fall from it, but to stir it up and grow in it, and to persevere in it unto the end of our lives; through Jesus Christ our Lord.

LANCELOT ANDREWES (1555–1626)

Blessings on a Church Congregation

Oh God, You who are in all places, when I meditate on what I will say and how I will say it, You are present; when the individual has resolved to come into Your house, You are present; but perhaps the thought is not truly present to him: Bless then this worship in order that each one of us individually will feel Your presence and know that we are before You. Amen.

SØREN KIERKEGAARD (1813–1855)

Look favorably upon every member of this congregation. Every day commit all of these human souls from the worst and weakest of hands into the best and strongest of hands—namely, your own.

FRIEDRICH VON BODELSCHWINGH
(19TH CENTURY)

———

Gather us, O Lord, as your Church members in the one great company of disciples, together following our Lord Jesus Christ into every walk of life; together serving him in his mission to the world; and together witnessing to his love throughout our life together. Amen.

———

Dear friends, I think of your insertion into the universal Church. It is a beautiful and great mystery. The tree of the Church, planted by Jesus in the Holy Land, has not stopped developing...and now your community of believers has in its turn been grafted onto the tree of the Church.

POPE JOHN PAUL II,
HOMILY IN THE CONGO, 1980

You, then, are my workers. You have come from me, the supreme eternal gardener, and I have engrafted you onto the vine by making myself one with you.

Keep in mind that each of you has your own vineyard. But every one is joined to your neighbor's vineyards without any dividing lines. They are so joined together, in fact, that you cannot do good or evil for yourself without doing the same for your neighbors.

All of you together make up one common vineyard, the whole Christian assembly, and you are all united in the vineyard of the mystic body of holy Church from which you draw your life. In this vineyard is planted the Vine, which is my only-begotten Son, into whom you must be engrafted.

SAINT CATHERINE OF SIENA (1347–1380)

Blessing on
the Church

Deliver your Church, Lord, from all evil
and teach it to love you perfectly.
You have made it holy.
Build it up from the four winds
And gather it into the kingdom
For which you have destined it.
Power and glory to you throughout the ages.

THE DIDACHE

Blessings on
a New Job or New Work

Bless _____ as he/she begins a new job and
give him/her the grace and strength to carry it
out. Bless us, help us to support one another in
our efforts and endeavors. Bless all who begin
new paths in daily work and living; guide them
in your truth. *Lord, hear us.*

THOMAS G. SIMONS

The things, good Lord, that we pray for, give us the grace to labor for.

SAINT THOMAS MORE (1478–1535)

Direct us, O Lord, in all our doings with your most gracious favor, and further us with your continual help; that in all our works begun, continued, and ended in you, we may glorify your holy Name, and finally, by your mercy, obtain everlasting life; through Jesus Christ our Lord. Amen.

THE BOOK OF COMMON PRAYER

O God, our comfort and challenge,
whose presence is ever reliable
and ever unexpected;
grant us to grieve over what is ending
without falling into despair
and to enter on our new vocation
without forgetting your voice,
through Jesus Christ our Lord. Amen.

JANET MORLEY

Blessing on
the Start of a New Project

You, O Judge of all the earth,
    Making the world stand firm by right
I pray to You, give life and pity
    Unto this people, humble in Your sight;
And set the prayer at morning light
    In place of sacrifice—
Even as the morning offering, the gift
    of every morn.
Make strong your hearts, my people,
    In God your strength; take courage true—
For if indeed you keep His statutes,
    He, setting love against the thing you do,
Will pardon your transgressions,
    Remembering in His wrath to pity you.
O seek the Lord, seek you His strength anew,
    Seek you His face for ever—
As with the morning offering, the gift
    of every morn.

SOLOMON BEN ABUN (12TH CENTURY)

Blessings for
Those Who Live Alone

Almighty God, whose Son had nowhere to lay his head: Grant that those who live alone may not be lonely in their solitude, but that, following in his steps, they may find fulfillment in loving you and their neighbors; through Jesus Christ our Lord. Amen.

TRADITIONAL PRAYER

———

Almighty God, our heavenly Father, who sets the solitary in families: We commend to thy continual care the homes in which your people dwell. Put far from them, we beseech you, every root of bitterness, the desire of vainglory, and the pride of life. Fill them with faith, virtue, knowledge, temperance, patience, godliness. Knit together in constant affection those who, in holy wedlock, have been made one flesh. Turn the hearts of the parents to the children, and the hearts of the children to the parents; and so enkindle fervent charity among us all, that we may evermore be kindly affectioned one to another; through Jesus Christ our Lord. Amen.

THE BOOK OF COMMON PRAYER

Blessings on the Death of a Loved One

Lord God,
you have made us mortal and we must die.
Do not, we beseech you,
take our lives away forever,
you who are a God of the living.
We ask you this for Jesus' sake,
today and every day,
for ever and ever.

HUUB OOSTERHUIS

———

O God, the Savior of both the living and the dying, I humbly beg you to pardon all my offenses, both those committed deliberately and those committed without thought and intention. And when at last you command that my soul should depart from my body, may your holy angels protect my soul from all evil powers, and carry it safely to your heavenly kingdom.

LEONINE SACRAMENTARY (5TH CENTURY)

I beseech you, good Jesus, that as you have graciously granted to me here on earth to enjoy the sweetness of your wisdom and truth, so at death you will bring me into your presence, that I may see the beauty of your face, and listen to your voice which is the source of all wisdom and truth.

THE VENERABLE BEDE (C. 673–735)

Blessings for the Poor

*T*he poor call to us. We have to be aware of them in order to love them. We have to ask ourselves if we know the truth. Do we know the poor in our own homes? Sometimes people can hunger for more than bread. Though it is possible, Lord, that our children, our husbands, our wives, do not hunger for bread, do not need clothes, do not lack a house, grant us the insight, though, to be sure that none of them feels alone, abandoned, neglected, or needing some affection. For that, too, is poverty.

MOTHER TERESA OF CALCUTTA (1910–1997)

You should be much more watchful than men of the world are, in order to turn your possessions to good use. Our possessions are not our own. God has given them to us so that we may cultivate them, and it is his will that we should make them useful and fruitful, so rendering him an acceptable service.

Self-love is violent, turbulent and restive, so that our cares on its behalf will be troubled, anxious and uneasy. The love of God is gentle, peaceful and tranquil, so that our cares springing from that source, although they concern worldly goods, will be gentle, mild and without anxiety.

However, it is as well to practice real practical poverty in the midst of the riches and advantages with which God has endowed you. Always dispose part of your means by giving alms freely to the poor, for you impoverish yourself of that which you give, and the more it is, the more you are impoverished.

Love poverty and the poor; for by this you will become truly poor yourself, since we become like that which we love.

SAINT FRANCIS DE SALES (1567–1622)

When poor people die of hunger, it has not happened because God did not take care of them. It has happened because neither you nor I wanted to give them what they needed. Give us the grace, O Lord, to be instruments of love in your hands to give the poor a piece of bread, to offer them clothes with which to ward off the cold. Help us to recognize Christ in them when, once more he appears under the guise of pain, when he is identified with a man numb from cold and dying of hunger, when he appears in the lonely form of a lost child in search of a home.

MOTHER TERESA OF CALCUTTA (1910–1997)

To matter in the scheme of the cosmos: this is better theology than all our sociology. It is, in fact, all that God has promised to us—that we matter. That he cares. As far as I know, no great prophet has promised people that God will give them social justice, though he may have threatened doom and extinction if the people themselves don't do something about it. If God cares about us, we have to care about each other.

MADELEINE L'ENGLE

Lover of the unlovable, we are captives of the world. Recapture our loyalties, not by defeating our will but by drawing it to yours. Seize our spirits, not by forcing us into your grasp but by freeing us from sin. Adore us, love us, desire and seek us. Our ears strain for the sound of you, our eyes for the sight of you; our hearts tremble in anticipation of your presence. Come into our midst, Lord, and make us your captives. Amen.

———

To allow the hungry to remain hungry would be blasphemy against God and one's neighbor, for what is nearest to God is precisely the need of one's neighbor. It is for the love of Christ, which belongs as much to the hungry as to myself, that I share my bread with them and that I share my dwelling with the homeless. If the hungry do not attain to faith, then the fault falls on those who refused them bread. To provide the hungry with bread is to prepare the way for the coming of grace.

DIETRICH BONHOEFFER (1906–1945)

O God the Father of everybody, you ask us all to bring love where the poor are humiliated, joy where the Church is downcast, and reconciliation where people are divided—fathers and sons, mothers and daughters, husbands and wives, believers and those who cannot believe, Christians and their unwanted fellow Christians. You open this way for us, so that the broken body of Jesus Christ, your Church, may be leaven of communion for the poor of the earth and in the whole human family.

BROTHER ROGER OF TAIZÉ

Blessings on Those Who Are Depressed

The breath of life, O Lord, seems spent.
My body is tense, my mind filled with anxiety,
Yet I have no zest, no energy.
I am helpless to allay my fears.
I am incapable of relaxing my limbs.
Dark thoughts constantly invade my head,
And I have no power to resist them....
Lord, raise up my soul, revive my body.

SAINT GREGORY OF NAZIANZUS (329?–390)

How rigid and inflexible I am! I can overcome my own stubbornness only with the greatest difficulty. And yet when I beg you for help, you seem to do nothing. Are you ignoring me on purpose? Are you waiting for me to take the thorns of sin from my flesh before you will assist me? Yes, I know I must dig out these thorns before they poison and destroy me completely. But I cannot do it without you.

SAINT HILDEGARD OF BINGEN (1098–1179)

Blessings for Saintliness

Eternal God, help us always to remember the great unseen saints round about us. When in danger, give us their courage, and when in difficulty, their perseverance; so that we too may be faithful until we rejoice with all the saints in your eternal kingdom, through Jesus Christ our Lord. Amen.

WILLIAM HAMPSON

O almighty God, who has called us to faith in You, and has compassed us about with so great a cloud of witnesses: Grant that we, encouraged by the good examples of Your Saints, may persevere in running the race that is set before us, until at length, through thy mercy, we with them attain to thine eternal joy; through him who is the author and finisher of our faith, thy Son Jesus Christ our Lord. Amen.

THE LESSER FEASTS AND FASTS

———

Unless the eye catch fire
    The God will not be seen.
Unless the ear catch fire
    The God will not be heard.
Unless the tongue catch fire
    The God will not be named.
Unless the heart catch fire
    The God will not be loved.
Unless the mind catch fire
    The God will not be known.

WILLIAM BLAKE (1757–1827)

Let believers on earth imitate the saints in heaven in nearness to Christ. Let us on earth be as the elders are in heaven, sitting around the throne. May Christ be the object of our thoughts and the center of our lives.

CHARLES SPURGEON (1834–1892)

Blessing on the Departed

God, who has authority over life and death, God of the spirits and Master of all flesh, God who deals out death and who gives life...who creates the spirit of man within him and takes to yourself the souls of the saints and gives them rest, who alters and changes and transforms your creatures, as is right and expedient, we beseech you for the repose and rest of this your servant [or this your handmaiden]: give rest to his soul, his spirit, in green places, in chambers of rest with Abraham and Isaac and Jacob and all your saints: and raise up his body in the day which you have ordained, according to your promises which cannot lie, that you may render to it also the heritage of which it is worthy

in your holy pastures. Remember not his transgressions and sins: and cause his going forth to
be peaceable and blessed. Heal the griefs of
those who still survive him with the spirit of
consolation, and grant unto us all a good end
through your only-begotten Son, Jesus Christ,
through whom is your glory and the strength
in the Holy Spirit to the age of the ages. Amen.

EUCHOLOGIUM OF SERAPION

Part V

Blessings
Through
the Seasons

Advent Blessings

Advent is a season for exiles. It is a time of waiting, a time of yearning for light to dispel the darkness....O God of exiles and strangers, find the homeless parts of me; guide them toward yourself, for you are my promised land. Take the stranger inside of me and find familiar soil for it. Keep me mindful of the Emmanuel, whose sojourn brought a glimpse of home.

JOYCE RUPP

———

The lowliness of Mary was made the heavenly ladder by which God descended upon earth. O true lowliness, which has borne God to man, has given life to mortals, opened the gates of paradise, and set free the souls of men.

SAINT AUGUSTINE (354–430)

———

When this old world drew on toward night,
you came; but not in splendor bright,
not as a monarch, but the child
of Mary, blameless mother mild...

"CREATOR OF THE STARS OF NIGHT"
(9TH CENTURY)

Above all, that birth at Bethlehem represents the culminating point of the history of salvation. From the moment of that birth on, the expectation was transformed into reality. The "Come!" of Advent meets with the "Here I am" of Bethlehem.

However, this primary perspective of birth is transformed into a further one. Advent not only prepares us for the birth of God who becomes man. It also prepares man for his own *birth from God*. Man must, in fact, constantly be born of God. His aspiration toward the truth, the good, the beautiful, the absolute, is actuated in this birth. When the night of Bethlehem comes, then Christmas day, the Church will say, at the sight of the Newborn, who will show weakness and insignificance, like every newborn child, "Any who did accept him *he empowered to become children of God*" (John 1:12).

POPE JOHN PAUL II

Blessing for
the Advent Wreath

O God, bless our wreath and be with us as we prepare our hearts for the coming of Christ. As we light the candle each day, help us to keep our own hearts burning with your love.

LIGUORI PUBLICATIONS PRAYER SERVICE

Blessing for the Lighting
of the Christmas Tree

Creator God, your own Son is the tender shoot that grew to become a majestic cedar. As birds find safety in giant branches, so we find shelter and comfort in your Son. We thank you for sending us Jesus, our Tree of Life.

Lord God, bless this tree in the name of the Father, and of the Son, and of the Holy Spirit. May it remind us throughout this holy season that Jesus is our Tree of Life. (*Turn on the lights.*) As we turn on the lights of our tree, we are reminded that Jesus is also the Light of our world. Amen.

LIGUORI PUBLICATIONS PRAYER SERVICE

Blessings for Christmas

Loving Father, as we think of the little Child of Bethlehem, make us glad that You the Almighty, the Creator, the Infinite, Whose Being is utterly beyond even the power of our loftiest thought and most daring imagination, can speak to us in a little human Child. Save us from being impressed too much by the impressive. Help us to see You in simple things: a child's life, birdsong, the quiet loveliness of dawn, human friendship and the peace of our homes. We bow in worship before the majesty of heaven revealed in a human life. Accept our worship and make our lives more like His. We ask it for His sake. Amen.

LESLIE D. WEATHERHEAD (1893–1976)

Immanuel, God with us in our nature, in our sorrow, in our lifework, in our punishment, in our grave, and now with us, or rather we with Him, in resurrection, ascension, triumph, and Second Advent splendor.

CHARLES H. SPURGEON (1834–1892)

Let us dance with delight in the Lord and let our hearts be filled with rejoicing, for eternal salvation has appeared on the earth, alleluia.

THE LITURGY OF THE HOURS, ROMAN RITE

O God, Who has made this most sacred night to shine with the illumination of the true Light; grant, we beseech You, that as we have known the mystery of that Light upon earth, we may also perfectly enjoy It in heaven.

COLLECT FOR MIDNIGHT MASS,
CHRISTMAS EVE

Sweet Child of Bethlehem, grant that we may share with all our hearts in this profound mystery of Christmas. Pour into our hearts the peace which we sometimes seek so desperately, and which you alone can give. Help us to know one another better and to live as brothers and sisters, children of the same Father. Awaken in our hearts love and gratitude for your infinite goodness; join us together in your love; and give us all your heavenly peace.

POPE JOHN XXIII (1881–1963)

Welcome, all wonders in one sight!
   Eternity shut in a span,
Summer in winter, day in night,
   Heaven in earth and God in man.
Great little one, whose all-embracing birth
Lifts earth to heaven, stoops heaven to earth.

RICHARD CRASHAW (1613?–1649),
"NATIVITY HYMN"

———

You have united, O Lord, your divinity with
our humanity and our humanity with your divinity, your life with our mortality and our mortality with your life. You have received what was
ours and given unto us what was yours.

SYRIAN LITURGY OF SAINT JAMES

———

Christ is born: give him glory!
Christ has come down from heaven:
   receive him!
Christ is now on earth: exalt him!
O you earth, sing to the Lord!
O you nations, praise him in joy,
   for he has been glorified!

CHRISTMAS CANON, ORTHODOX LITURGY

Hanukkah Blessings

Lord of Hosts, who is like unto You among the mighty? You alone are our strength and our song, an everpresent help in time of trouble. Though evil encamp against us, though hatred seek our downfall, we will recall Your victories of old, and trust in Your power.

On this day, glorified by ancient triumphs, we confess our weakness before You. We had believed in Your word, but disappointments have shaken our faith. We sought Your light, but despair has darkened our way. O be You our light and our salvation. Strengthen our hearts, for they are disquieted. Uplift our souls, for they are cast down. Some have forgotten Your word. Some are tempted to forsake Your worship. O grant that we and our household stand firm in battle. Teach us to rebuild the walls that are shattered. Teach us to cleanse the altars of our hearts, and to rededicate them this day to You, to Your service alone. Amen.

HANUKKAH PRAYER

Almighty God, you are the light of the world, grant us Your heavenly blessing. May the radiance of these lights, kindled in honor of this Festival, illumine our hearts, and brighten our home with the spirit of faith and love. Let the light of Your Presence guide us, for in Your light do we see light. Bless also with Your spirit the homes of all Israel and all mankind, that happiness and peace may ever abide in them. Amen.

JEWISH PRAYER FOR KINDLING THE LIGHTS

Kwanzaa Blessings

A BLESSING OF THE SEVEN GUIDING
PRINCIPLES: NGUZO SABA

For *Umoja* (Unity)...which is reflected in the
   African saying, "I am We," or "I am because
   We are."

For *Kujichagulia* (Self-Determination)...
   which requires that we define our common
   interests and make decisions in the best
   interest of family and community.

For *Ujima* (Collective Work and Responsibility)...which reminds us of our obligation to the past, present and future, and that we have a role to play in the community, society, world.

For *Ujamaa* (Cooperative Economics)... which emphasizes our collective economic strength and encourages us to meet common goals through mutual support.

For *Nia* (Purpose)...which helps us to build and maintain a strong and vibrant community.

For *Kuumba* (Creativity)...which makes use of our creative energies.

For *Imani* (Faith)...which focuses on honoring the best of our traditions, draws upon the best in ourselves, and helps us strive for a higher level of life for humankind, by affirming our self-worth and confidence in our ability to succeed and triumph in a righteous struggle.

*F*or the Motherland cradle of civilization.
For the ancestors and their indomitable spirit.
For the elders from whom we can
    learn much.
For our youth who represent the promise
    for tomorrow.
For our people the original people.
For our struggle and in remembrance of those who
have struggled on our behalf.
For *Umoja* the principle of unity which
    should guide us in all that we do.
For the creator who provides all things great
    and small.

LIBATION STATEMENT

Winter Blessings

O Lord, if it is not springtime in my chilly heart, I ask You to make it so. I am tired of living at a distance from You. This long, dreary winter, when will You end it? Come Holy Spirit, renew my soul! Make me alive! Restore me. Have mercy on me. Amen.

CHARLES SPURGEON (1834–1892)

Dews and falling snow, bless the Lord;
Sing praise to him and highly exalt
    him forever.
Ice and cold, bless the Lord;
Sing praise to him and highly exalt
    him forever.
Frosts and snows, bless the Lord;
Sing praise to him and highly exalt
    him forever.

PRAYER OF AZARIAH

Epiphany Blessings

If we do not believe, the waves engulf us, the
winds blow, nourishment fails, sickness lays us
low or kills us. If, on the other hand, we believe, the waters are welcoming and sweet, the
bread is multiplied, our eyes are open, the dead
rise again, the power of God is as it were drawn
from him by force and spreads throughout nature.

PIERRE TEILHARD DE CHARDIN (1881–1955)

Almighty God, our heavenly Father, Who has given us in Your Son Jesus Christ a fountain of life, which, springing up within us, can make all things new, we thank You for the deeper meaning which He gives to life—for the quickened sense of duty, the faith under sorrow, the immortal hopes, which we owe to Him. And we pray that His divine instructions may be so received by us with grateful hearts, that no resistance of ours may hinder His free working within us a miracle as when He changed the water into wine. In the power of His Spirit, may our griefs be transformed into consolations, our infirmities into strength to do well, our sins into repentance, our fainting and halting spirits into a heavenly mind; and, finally, the doubts, the discouragements, the trials of this earthly life, into the full assurance and unclouded bliss of an eternal life with You, through the same Jesus Christ our Lord. Amen.

HENRY W. FOOTE

Your epiphany, O Lord, made the earth leap for joy....The choir of shepherds on earth glorified thy all-saving advent. Today, the Word who sits on the throne of glory with the Father became flesh, born of the holy Virgin, giving the universe the grace of adoption.

SAINT EPHRAEM (4TH CENTURY)

———

Unclench your fists
Hold out your hands.
Take mine.
Let us hold each other.
Thus is his Glory
Manifest.

MADELEINE L'ENGLE

Lenten Blessings

Lord, for your tender mercy's sake lay not our sins to our charge; but forgive what is past, and give us grace to amend our sinful lives; to decline from sin, and incline to virtue, that we may walk in an upright heart before you this day and evermore.

CHRISTIAN PRAIERS AND
HOLY MEDITACIONS, 1568

You, the Life, were laid in the grave,
O Christ; and the hosts of the angels
shuddered, praising thy humility.

ORTHODOX RITE

Even though we are only dust and ashes, we must and we will "magnify the exceeding greatness of His grace." O heaven and earth, break forth in a song! Give all the glory, honor, and praise to our sweet Lord Jesus.

CHARLES SPURGEON (1834–1892)

O Savior, as thou hangest upon the tree,
I turn my back to thee but only to receive
Corrections, till thy mercies bid thee leave.
Oh think me worth thine anger, punish me,
Burn off my rusts and my deformity;
Restore thine image so much by thy grace,
That thou mayst know me—and I'll turn
  my face.

JOHN DONNE (1573–1631),
"GOOD FRIDAY RIDING WESTWARD"

———

Let us amend what we have
transgressed through ignorance,
lest, should the day of death suddenly
overtake us, we seek
time for repentance and cannot find it.
Hearken, O Lord, and have mercy, for we
have sinned against thee.
Help us, O God of our salvation,
and, for the glory
of thy name, deliver us.

WILLIAM BYRD (1543–1623),
RESPONSE AT ASH WEDNESDAY

All-seeing and ever-present God, no person slips through cracks in your perception and no event is slurred in the impeccable precision of your eternity. Make us all count to one another as seriously as we do to you; let not one of us given into your Son's care be lost, but bring us all to a share in his glory. Amen.

LINDA MURPHY, PRAYER FOR HOLY WEEK

God the Father, give us grace
To walk in the light
of Jesus' face;
God the Son give us
a part
In the hiding place of Jesus' heart.
God the Spirit so hold us up
That we may drink of Jesus' cup;
God Almighty, God
Three in One,
God Almighty, God
alone. Amen.

MATT TALBOT (1856–1925)

Where charity and love are found,
there is God.
The love of Christ has gathered us together
    into one.
Let us rejoice and be glad in him.
Let us fear and love the living God,
and love each other from the depths
    of our heart.
Therefore when we are together,
let us take heed not to be divided in mind.
Let there be an end to bitterness and quarrels,
    an end to strife,
and in our midst be Christ our God.
And, in company with the blessed, may we see
your face in glory, Christ our God,
pure and unbounded joy
for ever and ever.

PROCESSION WITH GIFTS FOR THE POOR,
HOLY THURSDAY, ROMAN RITE

Peter, Apostle, have you seen my love
   so bright?
I saw him with his enemies—
   a harrowing sight!

Who is that fine man upon the Passion Tree?
It is your Son, dear Mother, know you
   not me?

Is that the wee babe I bore nine months
   in my womb
That was born in a stable when no house
   would give us room?

Mother, be quiet, let not your heart be torn,
My keening women, Mother, are yet to
   be born!

Refrain: *M'ochon agus m'ochon o!*
   IRISH LAMENT

*I*n paradise of old the wood stripped
    me bare....
Now the wood of the cross that clothes us
    with the garment
    of life has been set up in the midst
    of the earth,
And the whole world is filled with
    boundless joy.
    EXALTATION OF THE CROSS,
    ORTHODOX LITURGY

———

*Y*ou taught us, Lord, that the greatest love a man can show is to lay down his life for his friends. But your love was greater still, because you laid down your life for your enemies. It was while we were still enemies that you reconciled us to yourself by your death. What other love has ever been, or could ever be, like yours? You suffered unjustly for the sake of the unjust. You died at the hands of sinners for the sake of the sinful. You became a slave to tyrants, to set the oppressed free.
    SAINT BERNARD OF CLAIRVAUX (1091–1153),
    HOLY WEEK PRAYER

Ascension Blessings

Lord, open our eyes to see the mighty change wrought by the ascension. Today tells us that God has committed all authority to His Son, so that in the very name of Jesus there is power.

WATCHMAN NEE, ADAPTED

O Christ, our God, the wisdom, power and glory of the Father, who did visibly appear to all men as the Word made flesh, and having overcome the prince of darkness, did return to your throne on high; Grant to us your supplicants, amid this dark world, the full outpouring of your splendor, and appoint the holy angels to be our defenders, to guard our going out and coming in, till we take our place at your right hand, where you live and reign with the Father and the Holy Ghost, ever one God, world without end.

MOZARABIC SACRAMENTARY

Lord Jesus, support those who hope in you, and give us your good counsel, so that we may know the joy of your Ascension and share the exaltation of the saints at your right hand, where you live and reign with the Father and the Holy Spirit, forever and ever. Amen.

———

To complete your seamless robe, and so to complete our faith, you ascended through the air of the heavens, before the very eyes of the apostles. In this way you showed that you are the Lord of all, and are the fulfillment of creation. Thus from that moment every human and every living creature should bow at your name. And, in the eyes of faith, we can see that all creation proclaims your greatness.

SAINT BERNARD OF CLAIRVAUX (1090–1153)

Rogation/Planting Blessings

Almighty God, Lord of heaven and earth: We beseech you to pour forth your blessing upon this land, and to give us a fruitful season; that we, constantly receiving your bounty, may evermore give thanks unto you in your holy Church; through Jesus Christ our Lord. Amen.

THE LESSER FEASTS AND FASTS

May we forge a new friendship
   with the natural world
and discover a new affinity with beauty,
   with life,
and with the Cosmic Christ in whom
   all things
were created
in heaven and on earth,
visible or invisible,
whether thrones or dominions
or principalities or authorities...
for all things were created through him
   and for him.
In his name. Amen.

CHINOOK PSALTER

Be a gardener.
Dig a ditch,
toil and sweat,
and turn the earth upside down
and seek the deepness
and water the plants in time.
Continue this labor
and make sweet floods to run
and noble and abundant fruits
to spring.
Take this food and drink
and carry it to God
as your true worship.

JULIAN OF NORWICH (C. 1342–AFTER 1413)

———

Lord, purge our eyes to see
Within the seed a tree.
Within the glowing egg a bird,
Within the shroud a butterfly.
Till, taught by such we see
Beyond all creatures, Thee....

CHRISTINA ROSSETTI (1830–1894)

Easter Blessings

I know that my Redeemer lives,
    Glory, hallelujah!
What comfort this sweet sentence gives,
    Glory, hallelujah!
Shout on, pray on, we're gaining ground.
    Glory, hallelujah!
The dead's alive, and the lost is found.
    Glory, hallelujah!
AMERICAN FOLK HYMN

Lord Jesus, our life and our resurrection, the tears you sowed in the sorrow of your Passion brought the earth to flower on Easter morning. Renew the wonders of your power in the church, so that, after the sorrows of our exile, we may come home to you in gladness and praise you now and forever. Amen.
LUTHERAN LITURGY

O faithful, come on this day of the glorious Resurrection: Let us drink the wine of the new vineyard, of the divine joy, of the Kingdom of Christ! Let us praise Christ as our God forever and ever. Amen.

EASTER SUNDAY ORTHODOX LITURGY

May the God who shakes heaven and earth, whom death could not contain, who lives to disturb and heal us, bless you with power to go forth and proclaim the gospel. Amen.

JANET MORLEY

At the latter day my redeemer shall stand upon the earth and mine eyes shall behold him and not as a stranger, but in the meantime I behold him on the earth as a name which when I write it wakes me up weeping, as a joke too rich to tell on certain silent faces, occasionally even my own face; as a hand which I am able sometimes to believe that only the thin glove of night I wear keeps me from touching.

FREDERICK BUECHNER

O Christ, you take upon yourself all our burdens so that, freed of all that weighs us down, we can constantly begin anew to walk, with lightened step, from worry towards trusting, from the shadows towards the clear flowing waters, from our own will towards the vision of the coming Kingdom. And then we know, though we hardly dared hope so, that you offer to make every human being a reflection of your face.

BROTHER ROGER OF TAIZÉ

Eternal Father, source of life and light,
whose love extends to all people,
all creatures, all things:
grant us that reverence for life
which becomes those who believe in you,
lest we despise it, degrade it,
or come callously to destroy it.
Rather let us save it, secure it,
and sanctify it, after the example
of your Son, Jesus Christ our Lord.

ROBERT RUNCIE

Spring Blessings

Christ keep the Hollow Land
Through the sweet springtide,
When the apple-blossoms bless
The lowly bent hill side.

Christ keep the Hollow Land
All the summertide;
Still we cannot understand
Where the waters glide;

Only dimly seeing them
Coldly slipping through
Many green-lipped cavern mouths
Where the hills are blue.

WILLIAM MORRIS (1834–1896)

Blessed are You, our God, Ruler of the universe. Your strength and power fill our world.

JEWISH PRAYER ON SEEING LIGHTNING
AND HEARING THUNDER

Deep peace of the running wave to you.
Deep peace of the flowing air to you.
Deep peace of the quiet earth to you.
Deep peace of the shining stars to you.
CELTIC BLESSING

———

Blessed are You, our God, Ruler of the universe:
Who made the big and beautiful sea...
Who created the fruit of the tree...
Who created all kinds of wonderful foods
for us to eat...
Who created the world with beauty big
and small
everywhere...
Who made the wonders of all creation.
TRADITIONAL JEWISH BLESSING

———

Dear Father,
Hear and bless
Your beasts
and singing birds:
And guard with tenderness
Small things
That have no words.

O Lord God of all creation, who stretched forth the heavens and laid the foundations of the earth, who has appointed the sun to rule by day, and the moon and stars to rule by night. You have set a boundary to the sea, and a law for the seasons have You ordained on high; the wind and the rain obey Your commands, and the dew of heaven descends at Your bidding to moisten the earth. In every time and season You have made manifest unto us Your wondrous works; and from festival to festival You have called us to invoke Your help in the sanctuary, and to praise You in public congregation; for You are gracious and beneficent. We come, therefore, this day to supplicate You, and to lay our petitions before the throne of Your glory.

JEWISH PRAYER FOR THE SEASONS

Grant me the ability to be alone;
may it be my custom to go outdoors each day
among the trees and grasses,
among all growing things,
and there may I be alone,
to talk with the one
that I belong to.

RABBI NACHMAN OF BRESLOV

Pentecost Blessings

O Holy Spirit of great power,
Come down upon us and subdue us;
From Your glorious mansion in the heavens
Your light effulgent shed on us.

Father beloved of every naked one,
From Whom all gifts and goodness come,
Our hearts illumine with Thy mercy,
In Thy mercy shield us from all harm.

The knee that is stiff; O Healer, make pliant,
The heart that is hard make warm beneath
    Thy wing;
The soul that is wandering from Thy path,
Grasp Thou his helm and he shall not die.

Each thing that is foul cleanse Thou each,
Each thing that is hard soften Thou with
    Thy grace,
Each wound that is aching in pain
O best of healers, make Thou whole!

TRADITIONAL GAELIC HYMN

O God the Holy Ghost...
Evermore enlighten us.
Thou who art Fire of Love,
Evermore enkindle us.
Thou who art Lord and Giver of Life,
Evermore live in us...
As the wind is Thy symbol,
So forward our goings.
As the dove,
So launch us heavenward...

CHRISTINA ROSSETTI (1830–1894)

May the God who dances in creation,
who embraces us with human love,
who shakes our lives like thunder,
bless us and drive us out with power
to fill the world with her justice. Amen.

JANET MORLEY

Christ is risen and you, death, are abolished.
Christ is risen and the demons are cast down,
Christ is risen and angels rejoice,
Christ is risen and life is freed,
Christ is risen and the tomb is emptied
   of the dead:
for Christ, being risen from the dead,
   has become the
Leader and Reviver of those who had
   fallen asleep.
To him be glory and power for ever and ever.

SAINT JOHN CHRYSOSTOM (345?–407)

Holy Spirit, Spirit of the Living God, you breathe in us on all that is inadequate and fragile. You make living water spring even from our hurts themselves. And through you, the valley of tears becomes a place of wellsprings. So, in an inner life, with neither beginning nor end, your continual presence makes new freshness break forth. Amen.

BROTHER ROGER OF TAIZÉ

Summer Blessing

All you big things, bless the Lord
Mount Kilimanjaro and Lake Victoria
The Rift Valley and the Serengeti Plain
Fat baobabs and shady mango trees
All eucalyptus and tamarind trees
Bless the Lord
Praise and extol Him for ever and ever.

All you tiny things, bless the Lord
Busy black ants and hopping fleas
Wriggling tadpoles and mosquito larvae
Flying locusts and water drops
Pollen dust and tsetse flies
Millet seeds and dried dagaa
Bless the Lord
Praise and extol Him for ever and ever.

TRADITIONAL AFRICAN PRAYER

Blessing for the Feast of the Trinity

All the feasts we have observed throughout this year, whatever they commemorated, have led up to this one feast and found their consummation in it, just as the course which creatures run has its goal and end in the Holy Trinity, for in a sense it is both beginning and end. When we come to speak of the Most Blessed Trinity, we are at a loss for words; and yet words must be used to say something for this sublime and ineffable Trinity. To express it adequately is as impossible as touching the sky with one's head. Yet to experience the working of the Trinity is better than to talk about it.

JOHANNES TAULER (1300?–1361)

Blessings for All Saints' Day

The glorious company of the apostles praise You. The goodly fellowship of the prophets praise You. The white-robed army of martyrs praise You. All Thy saints and elect with one voice do acknowledge You, O Blessed Trinity, one God!

ANTIPHON AT LAUDS, FEAST OF ALL SAINTS

O divine Saint-maker, Creator of all holiness, we pray today with those who have gone before us, to guide us in holiness and lead us to heaven. And we pray with those among us, whose lives and examples strengthen our communion with your Son Jesus and with all the faithful, who are your Church on earth. Amen.

LIGUORI PUBLICATIONS PRAYER SERVICE

Blessing for
All Souls' Day

Gentle Spirit of God, on this special day we remember our departed loved ones who dwell now in your glory. We loved them once with human love; we love them now in prayer and grace. Amen.

LIGUORI PUBLICATIONS PRAYER SERVICE

Harvest Blessings

Almighty God, Lord of heaven and earth, we humbly pray that your gracious care may give and preserve the seeds which we plant in our farms that they may bring forth fruit in good measure; that we who constantly receive from your goodness may always give thanks to you, the giver of all good things, through Jesus Christ, your Son, our Lord.

CAMEROON PRAYER USED DURING
THE PLANTING SEASON

Heavenly Sower, plow me first, and then sow the truth in me. Let me produce a bountiful harvest for You. Amen.

CHARLES SPURGEON (1834–1892)

———

Blessed are you, God of all creation
who give us abundantly of this harvest
thirty, sixty, and a hundredfold.
We praise you for the blessings of
     food and drink
For provision for another year
For health and salvation.
Strengthen us, as we reap these benefits,
to enjoy your goodness
and to give of our bounty to help the
     poor and needy.

———

Bless us, dark earth as we give back
that which we have received
As we make a forest of blessing
a ridge of blessing
for the future to grow upon.

CHINOOK PSALTER

215

We beseech thee, Almighty God, to bless this crop of new apples, that we, who are doomed to a just sentence of death, by our first parents' eating of this deadly tree and fruit, may all be sanctified and blessed through the intercession of your only Son, our Redeemer, the Lord Jesus Christ, and by the benediction of the Holy Spirit. And, the wicked deceits of the Temptor of that first crime being averted, may we from this day—the solemn anniversary of Saint James—undertake in health the eating of these new fruits, through God in his unity.

OLD SARUM RITE FOR THE "CHRISTENING"
OF THE NEW APPLES

For the fruits of creation, thanks be to God!
For unique gifts to every nation, thanks
    be to God!
For the plowing, sowing, reaping
Silent growth while we are sleeping,
Future needs in earth's safekeeping, thanks
    be to God!
For the harvests of God's Spirit, thanks
    be to God!

For the good we all inherit, thanks be to God!
For the wonders that astound us,
For the truths that still confound us,
Most of all that love has found us, thanks
    be to God!

————

Blessings for Patriotic Occasions

The natural equality of human beings
    among each other must be duly favored,
in that government was never established by
    God nor nature
to give one person a prerogative to insult
    over another....
The end of all good government is to
    promote the happiness
of all and the good of all people
in all their rights to life, liberty, estate, honor,
without injury or abuse to any.

JOHN WISE (1652–1725)

O eternal God, through whose mighty power our fathers won their liberties of old: Grant, we beseech you, that we and all the people of this land may have grace to maintain these liberties in righteousness and peace; through Jesus Christ our Lord. Amen.

THE LESSER FEASTS AND FASTS

Blessings for Good Government

O God, source of all authority
  in the nations and the world,
help us to make and keep this country
a welcome home for all of its peoples;
and grant to our nation and
  all its representatives
imagination, skill, and energy
that peace and unity and justice may rule.

Eternal God, Lord of wisdom
we ask you to bless the representatives
that we have elected.
May they learn in honesty and integrity
to solve our problems
and to build toward the future
well-being of our nation. Amen.

———

Almighty God, who has given us this good land for our heritage: We humbly ask that we may always prove ourselves a people mindful of your favor and glad to do your will. Bless our land with honorable industry, sound learning, and pure manners. Save us from violence, discord, and confusion; from pride and arrogance, and from every evil way. Defend our liberties, and fashion into one united people the multitudes brought here out of many kindred and tongues. Endue with the spirit of wisdom those to whom in your Name we entrust the authority of government, that there may be justice and peace at home, and that, through obedience to your law, we may show forth your praise among the nations of the earth. In the time of prosperity, fill our hearts with thankfulness, and in the day of trouble, do not allow our trust in you to fail; all this we ask through Jesus Christ our Lord. Amen.

THE BOOK OF COMMON PRAYER

O Lord, our Governor, bless the leaders of our land, that we may be a people at peace among ourselves and a blessing to other nations of the earth.

Lord, keep this nation under your care.

To the President and members of the Cabinet, to Governors of States, Mayors of Cities, Senators and Representatives, officers of the Court, and all in administrative authority, grant wisdom and grace in the exercise of their duties.

Give grace to your servants, O Lord.

And, we pray, teach our people to rely on your strength and to accept their responsibilities to their fellow citizens, that they may elect trustworthy leaders and make wise decisions for the well-being of our society. And may we serve you faithfully in our generation and honor your holy name.

For yours is the kingdom, O Lord, and you are exalted as head above all. Amen.

Blessing for the Armed Forces

God, our stronghold and defense
we commend to you today those whose task it is
to defend us in times of danger.
Inspire them in war to serve our country well.
In peace, hold them ready and alert.
Bless them as they protect and preserve
    the innocent.
In their lives may they bring honor to our
    country's name.
Amen.

Thanksgiving Blessings

Let us praise Him with our lips, and laud and
magnify His name, from whose bounty all this
goodness flows. Then let us glorify God by
yielding our gifts to His cause....

We thank God for what we have, but we long
for more. When shall we see God and Jesus, and
heaven and truth, face to face?

CHARLES SPURGEON (1834–1892)

Blessed are you, God of the universe.
You have created us and given us life.
Blessed are the people who enjoy this land
who live and breathe freedom
and who have the resources to continue
in work and in love by your grace.
May our circle of freedom expand
to bring life to others;
and preserve us as we seek to do your will.
Amen.

———

Gratitude is the praise we offer God:
   for teachers kind,
   benefactors never to be forgotten,
   for all who have advantaged me,
   by writings, sermons, converse,
   prayers, examples,
   for all these and all others,
   which I know, which I know not,
   open, hidden,
   remembered, and forgotten.
LANCELOT ANDREWES (1555–1626)

On this Thanksgiving Day, as we gather in the warmth of our families, in the mutual love and respect which we have for one another, and as we bow our heads in submission to divine Providence, let us...pray for His divine wisdom in banishing from our land any injustice or intolerance or opposition to any of our fellow Americans, whatever the color of their skins, for God made all of us, not some of us, in His image. All of us, not just some of us, are His children.

LYNDON B. JOHNSON (1908–1973),
THANKSGIVING PRAYER

You have given so much to me
Give one thing more—a grateful heart:
Not thankful when it pleases me,
As if your blessings had spare days,
But such a heart whose pulse may be
Your Praise alone.

GEORGE HERBERT (1593–1633)

Eternal Spirit of Justice and Love,

At this time of Thanksgiving we would be aware of our dependence on the earth and on the sustaining presence of other human beings, both living and gone before us. As we partake of bread and wine, may we remember that there are many for whom sufficient bread is a luxury, and for whom wine, when attainable, is only an escape. Let our thanksgiving for Life's bounty include a commitment to changing the world, that those who are now hungry may be filled and those without hope may be given courage. Amen.

CONGREGATION OF ABRAXAS

Blessing for
New Year's Eve

O Lord, our Father! We have gathered here at the turn of the year because we do not want to be alone but want to be with each other, and together be united with you. Our hearts are filled with somber thoughts as we reflect on our misdeeds of the past year. And our ears are deafened by the voices of the radio and in the newspapers with their numerous predictions for the coming year. Instead we want to hear your word, your voice, your assurance, your guidance. We know that you are in our midst, and are eager to give us all that we need, whether we ask or not. On this night we ask for one thing only: that you collect our scattered thoughts, getting rid of the confused and defiant thoughts that may distract us, and thus enable us to concentrate on your limitless generosity to us. You were abundantly generous to us last year, and will be no less generous to us next year, and in every year to come. Fill us with gratitude to you.

KARL BARTH (1886–1968)

Part VI

Select Resources
and Acknowledgments

SELECT RESOURCES AND ACKNOWLEDGMENTS

Grateful thanks and acknowledgment is made to authors and publishers for the use of the following material. Every effort has been made to contact original sources. However, any omissions should be brought to the attention of the publisher for correction in future editions.

An African Prayer Book, selected and with introduction by Desmond Tutu (New York: Doubleday), 1995.

All Desires Known, Janet Morley (Ridgefield, Conn.: Morehouse Publishing), 1988, 1992. "O God our comfort and challenge," "May the God who shakes heaven and earth," and "May the God who dances in creation," © Janet Morley, reprinted by permission of Morehouse Publishing.

The Alphabet of Grace, Frederick Buechner (San Francisco: HarperSanFrancisco), 1989. "At the latter day my redeemer shall stand," © 1970 by Frederick Buechner. Reprinted by permission of HarperCollins Publishers, Inc.

The Alternative Service Book, Anglican Church of Canada (William Collins), 1909.

Are You Running With Me, Jesus, Malcolm Boyd (Boston: Beacon Press), 1990.

Baha'i Prayers, (Wilmette, Ill.: Baha'i Publishing Trust), © 1954, 1982, 1985 by the National Spiritual Assembly of the Baha'is of the U.S.

Blessing and Praise: A Book of Meditations and Prayers for Individual and Home Devotion, (Cincinnati: Central Conference of American Rabbis), 1923.

Blessings for God's People, Thomas G. Simons (Notre Dame, Ind.: Ave Maria Press), 1959. "Summer has been," "God, ever generous," and "Bless _____ as he/she begins a new job" excerpted from *Blessings for God's People* by Thomas G. Simons. Copyright 1995 by Ave Maria Press, Notre Dame, Indiana. Used with permission of the publisher.

The Book of Common Prayer (New York: The Church Pension Fund), 1945.

A Book of Everyday Prayers, William Barclay (New York: Harper & Row), 1959. Used by permission.

The Book of Hours, © 1985, The Congregation of Abraxas, a Unitarian Universalist Order for Liturgical and Spiritual Renewal.

A Chain of Prayer Across the Ages, compiled by Selina Fox, (London: John Murray), 1913.

Children's Prayers From Around the World, Mary Batchelor (Minneapolis: Augsburg), 1955.

Christmas: A Christmas Sourcebook (Chicago: Archdiocese of Chicago), 1984, edited by Mary Ann Simcoe.

A Circle of Quiet, Madeleine L'Engle (New York: Farrar, Strauss), 1971. Used by permission.

The Communion of Saints: Prayers of the Famous, edited by Horton Davis, (Grand Rapids, Mich.: William B. Eerdmans), 1990.

The Complete Book of Christian Prayer (New York: Continuum), 1997.

Divine Milieu: An Essay on the Interior Life (New York: HarperCollins), 1975. Pierre Teilhard De Chardin.

Dolores Curran on Family Prayer (Mystic, Conn.: Twenty-Third Publications), 1997. Copyright Dolores Curran, reprinted by permission of Twenty-Third Publications, Mystic, CT 06366, toll free: 1-800-321-0411. Further reproduction without permission is prohibited.

The Doubleday Prayer Collection, compiled by Mary Batchelor (New York: Doubleday), 1992, 1996.

Early Christian Prayers (Chicago: Henry Regnery Company), 1961, edited by A. Hamman, O.F.M.

Earth Prayers From Around the World, edited by Elizabeth Roberts and Elias Amidon (San Francisco: HarperSanFrancisco), 1991.

The HarperCollins Book of Prayers, edited by Robert Van de Weyer (San Francisco: Harper SanFrancisco), 1993.

His Thoughts Said...His Father Said, Amy Carmichael (Fort Washington, Penn.: Christian Literature Crusade), 1941.

Hold Me Close, Ruth Harms Calkin (Wheaton, Ill.: Tyndale House), 1996. Used by permission.

The Hungering Dark, Frederick Buechner (New York: The Seabury Press), 1969. "Lord, catch us off guard," copyright © 1969 by Frederick Buechner. Reprinted by permission of Harper-Collins Publishers, Inc.

The Irrational Season, Madeleine L'Engle (New York: The Seabury Press), 1977. Used by permission.

Islamic Spirituality I, edited by Seyed H. Nasr (New York: Crossroad), 1987.

Laughter, Silence & Shouting, Kathy Keay (New York: HarperCollins), 1994.

The Lesser Feasts and Fasts, (New York: The Church Pension Fund), 1963.

Let's Begin With Prayer, Mitch Finley (Notre Dame, Ind., Ave Maria Press), 1977. "God of play," "God of games and play," and "God, our loving father" excerpted from *Let's Begin With Prayer* by Mitch Finley, copyright 1997 by Ave Maria Press. Used with permission of the publisher.

The Manual of Catholic Prayer, edited by H. P. R. Finberg (New York: Harper & Row), 1961.

May I Have This Dance, Joyce Rupp (Notre Dame, Ind.: Ave Maria Press), 1992.

Meditations, Dorothy Day (Mawah, N.J.: Paulist Press), 1970.

Meditations and Devotions, John Henry Newman, (London & New York: Longmans, Green), 1903.

Morning and Evening, Charles H. Spurgeon (Nashville, Tenn.: Thomas Nelson, Inc.), 1994, edited by Roy H. Clarke.

Meditations on the Way of the Cross, Mother Teresa of Calcutta and Brother Roger of Taizé (New York: Pilgrim Press), 1987.

Mother Teresa: In My Own Words, José Luis González-Balado, (Liguori, Mo.: Liguori Publications), 1996. Used by permission.

A New Zealand Prayer Book: He Karakia Mihinare O Aotearoa, Church of the Province of New Zealand (San Francisco: HarperSanFrancisco), 1989.

Out of Solitude, Henri J. M. Nouwen (Notre Dame, Ind.: Ave Maria Press), 1974.

The Oxford Book of Prayer (Oxford University Press), 1985.

Plain Prayers in a Complicated World, Avery Brooke (Boston: Cowley Publications), 1993. Used by permission.

Pope John Paul II: Prayers and Devotions (Chicago: Regnery Gateway), 1984. "Above all, that birth at Bethlehem."

Power Strategies of Jesus Christ, Harry A. Olson (Tarrytown, N.Y.: Triumph Books), 1991. Used by permission.

Prayer: Finding the Heart's True Home, Richard J. Foster (San Francisco: HarperSanFrancisco), 1992.

Prayers: Ancient and Modern, Mary W. Tileston (Boston: Little Brown and Company), 1908.

Prayers and Devotions from Pope John Paul II, edited by Peter van Lierde, O.S.A., (New York: Viking), 1994.

Prayers for the Domestic Church: A Handbook for Worship in the Home, Edward Hays (Leavensworth, Kans.: Forest of Peace Publishing), 1979. Used by permission.

The Prayers of Kierkegaard (Chicago: University of Chicago Press), 1956, edited by Perry D. LeFevre.

The Priest's Prayer Book (London: Joseph Masters), 1865.

The Raccolta: Prayers and Devotions (Boston: Benziger Brothers Inc.), 1944, edited by Joseph P. Christopher and Charles E. Spence.

Seeking God, Esther de Waal (London: Faith Press), 1984.

Strength to Love, Martin Luther King, Jr. (Philadelphia: Fortress Press), 1963.

Song of the Sparrow: Meditations and Poems to Pray By, Murray Bodo, O.F.M. (Cincinnati: Saint Anthony Messenger Press), 1979. Used by permission.

Thoughts in Solitude, Thomas Merton (San Francisco: HarperSanFrancisco), 1992.

Spiritual Life (Washington, D.C.: Washington Province of Discalced Carmelite Friars), Summer 1996.

A Triduum Sourcebook, Gabe Huck and Mary Ann Simcoe (Chicago: Archdiocese of Chicago), 1983.

The Way of the Heart, Henri J. M. Nouwen (New York: The Seabury Press), 1981.

Weavings, March/April 1997, (Nashville: The Upper Room), "Loving Christ, you who were not minded to cling to eternal glory," a poem by Glenn Hinson. Used by permission.

Whistling in the Dark, Frederick Buechner (San Francisco: HarperSanFrancisco), 1993. "Literature, painting, music," copyright © 1963 by Frederick Buechner. Reprinted by permission of HarperCollins Publishers, Inc.

The Wisdom of John Paul II: The Pope on Life's Most Vital Questions, compiled by Nick Bakalar and Rich Balkan (New York: HarperCollins), 1995.

Wishful Thinking: A Theological ABC, Frederick Buechner (San Francisco: HarperSanFrancisco), 1993. "Have you wept at anything," copyright © 1973 by Frederick Buechner. Reprinted by permission of HarperCollins Publishers, Inc.

With One Voice: Prayers From Around the World, compiled by Robert Bartlett (New York: T. Y. Crowell Company), 1961.

A World At Prayer: The New Ecumenical Prayer Cycle, compiled by John Carden and the World Council of Churches (Mystic, Conn.: Twenty-Third Publications), 1990.